SENATOR

A PROFILE OF BILL BRADLEY IN THE U.S. SENATE

SENATOR

A PROFILE OF BILL BRADLEY IN THE U.S. SENATE

WILLIAM JASPERSOHN

Harcourt Brace Jovanovich, Publishers

SAN DIEGO   NEW YORK   LONDON

HBJ

Picture credits: 1961 Crystal City High School Yearbook, Crystal City, MO.: p. 9, 13; courtesy
Princeton University Sports Information Director's Office: p. 15; Gerry Cranham/*Sports Illustrated:*
p. 18; courtesy Basketball Hall of Fame, Springfield, MA: p. 20; Wide World Photos: p. 22;
courtesy United States Senate Historian's Office: p. 26 (top), 30, 32, 35; courtesy John Dèspres/
Senate Staff: pp. 93, 96 (bottom); courtesy Greg Guroff/USIA: p. 96 (top).
All other photographs by the author.

Library of Congress Cataloging-in-Publication Data
Jaspersohn, William.
Senator: a profile of Bill Bradley in the U.S. Senate/William Jaspersohn.
p.   cm.
Includes bibliographical references and index.
Summary: Text and photographs reveal the background and
day-to-day life of Senator Bill Bradley, both on Capitol Hill
and among his constituents in New Jersey.
ISBN 0-15-272880-5
1. Bradley, Bill, 1943–   —Juvenile literature.   2. Legislators—United States—Biography—
Juvenile literature.   3. United States. Congress. Senate—Biography—Juvenile literature.
1. Bradley, Bill, 1943– . 2. Legislators.]   I. Title.
E840.8.B67J37   1992
328.73'092—dc20   91-11668
[B]

Designed by Trina Stahl
Printed in the United States of America
First edition
A B C D E

For Grace Helen Quinlan

and the EVs

CONTENTS

INTRODUCTION

I FIRST MET BILL Bradley in June 1967, in the publicity office at
the old Madison Square Garden on Eighth Avenue in New York
City. Bill was twenty-three, a recent Oxford graduate who had
just signed a half-million-dollar contract to play professional basketball for the New York Knickerbockers; I was nineteen, a student at Dartmouth (where I had invited Bill to speak that fall)
and a budding free-lance writer wishing to interview him for a
potential magazine story. As Bill's appointed arrival time came
and went, the two Knicks publicists present began going quietly
crazy. "This guy's gonna be trouble," one of them muttered. When
two hours later an apologetic Bill Bradley phoned to report that
his Volkswagen had broken down on the Long Island Expressway,
the other publicist said, "Good. Maybe now we can get him to
buy a new car."

"I don't think so," said the first. "Cars don't really interest
him."

Neither did clothes, apparently. When Bill arrived some three hours late, I noticed that his shoes were scuffed, his jacket was missing a button, and his shirt was torn at the shoulder. None of that seemed to matter to him. With his infamous left eyebrow arching earnestly, his long-fingered hands lofting imaginary basketballs in front of his face, he apologized for missing our appointment, then quickly discussed with me the topic for his Dartmouth talk: social responsibility. I found him to be serious, polite, friendly, a good listener. When our few minutes together were up, he scribbled down his phone number and invited me to call so we could continue talking.

What interested me then about Bill, and still interests me today, is his unceasing drive for personal excellence. With monkish determination and self-discipline he had become one of college basketball's greatest players, and the ten years that lay ahead of him as a Knick would earn him a place in the Basketball Hall of Fame. What I didn't know that hot June morning was that, in characteristically deliberate fashion, Bill was also beginning to prepare himself for a possible career after pro basketball, in politics. That preparation seems to me now, in retrospect, consistent with the remarks he made that fall to a packed student audience at Dartmouth: how we each have it in us to make a difference in our society; how poverty and ignorance are a waste of human potential; how service to our fellow mortals is humankind's highest calling.

Years passed. I stayed abreast of Bill's basketball career (and then, after his election to the U.S. Senate in 1978, his political career) with the interest of one who has met the person behind the headlines. In 1988, having written a handful of "day in the life" books for young people on different professions, I felt drawn to the notion of doing one on an elected official. There was really no question in my mind about who my subject would be. I phoned Bill's Senate office in October 1988, and a young press aide named

Greg McCarthy took my name and told me he would review my
request with the senator.

Seven months later, I found myself meeting Bill again, this
time at Middlebury College, Vermont, where he was scheduled to
deliver the commencement address. He was friendly and curious.
Yes, he remembered his visit to Dartmouth, he said, and he asked
me what I had been doing since we had last seen each other. He
told me to get in touch with him through his press office in
Washington and indicated he looked forward to being the subject
of my book. As we had earlier agreed, I would have access to his
day-to-day senatorial activities, though not unlimited access—certain aspects of his work, such as his membership on the Senate
Intelligence Committee, were necessarily off-limits to me (and, I
might add, to most of his staff), as were sensitive policy discussions
with staff and colleagues. I would check facts with him and his
staff, but editorial control of the book itself was mine alone. I
could interview whomever I pleased; indeed, no one I asked—
including Bill's closest friends and advisors—refused to talk to
me.

Over an eighteen-month period I observed Bill in the Senate
chamber, in his office, and at numerous functions around Washington and in New Jersey. I rode the Senate subway with him,
rattled along the New Jersey coastline in a van with him, ate in
restaurants with him, toured lighthouses, factories, boardwalks,
schools, and nursing homes with him, watched him meet everyone
from movie starlets to fire fighters to leading Russian economists.
I also had the opportunity to observe firsthand many of his campaign activities for election to a third term in the Senate.

If anything emerges from this portrait, I hope it is the kalei-
doscopic, exhausting, and often harrowing nature of the job of
senator, as well as the dedication and integrity of the portrait's
subject. My happiest discovery during the time I spent with Bill
is that he is, in fundamental ways, the same person he was back

in 1967. The English poet William Wordsworth once wrote, "The child is father of the man." He might have been writing about William Warren Bradley.

William Jaspersohn
Johnson, Vermont
September 8, 1991

SENATOR

A PROFILE OF BILL BRADLEY IN THE U.S. SENATE

Senator Bill Bradley (*center*) in the commencement procession at Middlebury College

1

COMMENCEMENT

On a breezy day in late May, New Jersey's senior senator, Bill Bradley, walks in a procession on the campus of Middlebury College in Middlebury, Vermont. Over his navy blue suit and sleeveless navy sweater he wears a black graduation robe and mortarboard cap because today is Commencement Day at Middlebury, and Bill is an honorary degree recipient and the featured speaker.

"What do you think of those Pistons?" a faculty member asks him in reference to Detroit's basketball team, which has made the NBA finals.

"I think they've got a good shot at it," replies Bill, himself a former professional basketball player for the New York Knickerbockers.

"We'd better be quiet now," the faculty person whispers, as the college orchestra near the commencement stage begins playing the graduation march.

The stage, Middlebury College, commencement

A few minutes later, Bill finds himself seated on the stage along with Middlebury officials and today's other honorary degree recipients. Before him, seated in folding chairs on the vast green lawn, are the five-hundred-plus Middlebury seniors who will receive their bachelor of arts degrees this morning, and their parents and families, who have come to celebrate with them.

The senator stifles a yawn. Three days earlier he delivered a commencement address at a college in Pennsylvania, and tomorrow he will do the same at Rutgers University in New Jersey. Such requests are a common feature of being a United States senator, and typically Bill accepts two or three each spring, but they take their toll on him. To fulfill today's commitment, for example, he rose before dawn at his home in Denville, New Jersey, gulped a muffin and coffee for breakfast, and at 6 A.M. a member of his staff drove him to Newark Airport, where a Learjet, paid for by Middlebury College, flew him to Rutland, Vermont, a few miles south of the campus. From there a delegation of Middlebury officials drove him to the campus in time for today's ceremonies at ten o'clock.

Now the president of Middlebury introduces Bill, and after a round of applause, the senator begins his speech. He congratulates the seniors and their parents on their achievement and asks the parents of the graduates to stand and be recognized. The audience applauds and cheers. Then, after telling a few jokes about himself and his lackluster taste in clothes, he launches into the body of his address. He says that the world—especially the Soviet Union and Eastern Europe—is changing and that America is in a position to "define who we are, what we believe in, and offer the world a positive new vision.

"What should be the goal for American society?" Bill answers his question in one word: *excellence*. "America should have a big ambition," he says. "Why not every person in America healthy and educated, an athlete of the body and Aristotle of the mind? . . . Today, the need to realize our human potential may very well be the key to our economic and political future in a competitive world. Just think: every American mother who can't afford prenatal care; every ten-year-old who doesn't have enough to eat; every teenager who can't read the instructions on a frozen food package, much less on a job application; every life wasted by drugs—these mean America not only is less than it could be, but less than we need to be.

"Today, in a world with a global economy and a global ecology, our national goal must be excellence."

The graduates, who have been loud and raucous all morning, sit silently, listening closely to the address. Bill Bradley does not have a natural speaking voice—it can sound dry and husky. But today, he compensates for this deficiency with his eloquence and passion. He says, "I believe that the ultimate challenge posed to a citizen of a democracy is to ask yourself what you owe another human being. By this, I don't mean what you owe yourself or your family or your friends, but rather what you owe a stranger simply because he or she is a part of the *human community*. Each of us, alone with our conscience and our intellect, determines what we owe to starving Ethiopians, to refugees from tyranny, to the deinstitutionalized homeless who sleep on the streets of our major cities. My life has told me that I do owe another human being. And I owe him more than charity or taxes. I owe him a part of my life. That's why I'm in politics."

Bill closes with a story that he hopes will illustrate his point. "Erma Bombeck tells the story of a successful career woman who decides she's had enough making money and wants to give something back. She asks, How? Who? Where? And in her puzzling, she writes Mother Teresa in Calcutta and offers to volunteer and seeks her advice. Weeks pass—finally a letter. She opens it and

"So I say to each of you . . . find your own Calcutta."

Mother Teresa has a one-sentence reply: 'Thank you for your offer, but find your own Calcutta.' "

Find your own Calcutta. Bill pauses, letting those words sink in. With a ring of challenge in his voice he says, "So I say to each of you . . . *find your own Calcutta.*"

The audience listens, stunned.

"It's around you every day. And then after you've found it— give some time through your job, or through volunteer work— to make things better. To help another human being."

There is honesty in the husky voice, and thoughtfulness, and a plea, and there is the sense that a complex man is revealing his innermost feelings.

"Nothing is more fulfilling. Nothing is more necessary to solve many of today's problems. Nothing is more essential to realize the potential of your own humanity. Thank you."

"My life has told me that I do owe
another human being. And I owe
him more than charity or taxes. I
owe him a part of my life. That's
why I'm in politics."

Silence. No one in the audience moves. Then, like rain falling, the applause begins, building steadily until, after a few seconds, it cascades across the bright lawn in long, sustained sheets. Students stand and keep applauding, and Bill, who has sat down, rises again and dips his head in quiet acknowledgment. He considers a commencement address an opportunity to communicate a message. Judging from the response of this gathering, his message has made an impact.

"THANKS A LOT FOR coming."

"I really dug your speech."

"Can I have your autograph?"

After the commencement ceremonies, people press around Bill, thrusting programs at him to sign, introducing their children, telling him that, if he ever runs for president of the United States, they'll vote for him. Since his undergraduate days at Princeton, he has been touted for the presidency, and he has grown used to people confronting him with the idea. Now he says thank you to all the well-intentioned remarks, and before long his hosts are signalling him that it is time to go. A few hours later he is back in New Jersey, and the next day, Washington, D.C., where work awaits him in his job as a United States senator.

2

BACKGROUND

WHEN BILL BRADLEY WAS growing up, his father wanted him to be a gentleman and his mother wanted him to be a success. He was born William Warren Bradley on July 28, 1943, in Crystal City, Missouri, a small town situated between two limestone bluffs thirty miles below St. Louis on the banks of the Mississippi River. His father, Warren Bradley, was a dignified man, the town bank president and a nominal Republican. He was, and still is, prosperous, but he knew hard times as a boy. His own father died when he was nine. He had to quit high school in the tenth grade and take a job as a ticket taker for the local railroad to help his family make ends meet. Later he worked at the Crystal City State Bank of which, in sixteen years, he became president. Reading helped the senior Bradley compensate for his lack of formal schooling, and in his son he instilled the value of education and hard work. He could not play sports with young Bill; a painfully arthritic

Bill Bradley as a senior at Crystal City High School, Crystal City, Missouri, June 1961

back made even walking difficult for him. And besides, to Warren Bradley, sports, though an acceptable part of a young man's life, were less important than pursuing a respectable career—in banking, say, or business, or law.

Bill's mother, Susan Crowe Bradley, has always been an energetic woman. Tall, athletic, determined, enthusiastic, a Cub Scout den mother and a Sunday-school teacher, she felt that her son could best learn how to do things by taking lessons. So young Bill took them. Dancing, boxing, golf, swimming, tennis, typing, riding, French horn ("I was the tallest French horn player in the school marching band," he says). His mother told John McPhee, Bill's first biographer, "I wanted a Christian upright citizen, and I thought the best way to begin was by promoting things that would interest a little boy."

"It was a reserved house, highly structured," Bill said much later. "Not strict in the sense of heavy discipline, but there wasn't much time for loose easiness, either. It was always this lesson or that, and schoolwork."

The senior Bradleys still live in the same tan brick ranch house on Taylor Avenue, across the street from the Grace Presbyterian Church. As the only child of the only bank president in Crystal City, Bill would sometimes encounter resentment from other boys when he tried to enter pickup football games in the churchyard. "This was something that hurt me in a very personal way," he later told McPhee. "They would not judge me for what I was." Once, in the schoolyard when he was around ten, Bill found himself surrounded by a group of older boys who beat his bare legs with switches and shouted at him, "Dance, banker's son, dance!" Another older boy heard the ruckus and chased the bullies away, but incidents such as these stayed with young Bill. He grew up feeling somewhat apart from other boys, and that he needed to prove that he was more than just "the banker's son."

Fortunately, he had athletic ability and, with it, a more intangible quality: leadership. When he was nine, he started playing basketball at the local YMCA, and his mother, noting his enthusiasm for the game, bolted a basket on the side of the garage so he and his fellow Cub Scouts could play after den meetings. In Little League he was a solid hitter and a sound first baseman. "You could tell Bill was going to be an athlete," says Dick Cook, a longtime friend. "And he showed leadership qualities even then. It wasn't a bullying kind of leadership, either. He led by example."

Bill's enthusiasm for basketball blossomed into full-blown passion—in part because he discovered the game on his own, in part because he was good at it. The problem was, every winter his parents spent two months in Palm Beach, Florida, and Bill felt as much an outsider there as back home in Crystal City. Also, the Palm Beach Private School, which Bill attended, emphasized soccer, fencing, and boxing, not basketball. So, with his own ball brought from home, Bill practiced every day in a public playground a few blocks from the hotel where he and his parents stayed. Sometimes he was joined by local boys, whom he befriended; mostly, however, he practiced alone. "What attracted me," he told John McPhee, "was the sound of the swish, the sound of the dribble, the feel of going up in the air. You don't need eight others, like in baseball. You don't need any brothers or sisters. Just you. I wonder what the guys are doing back home. I'd like to be there, but it's as much fun here, because I'm playing. It's getting dark. I have to go back for dinner. I'll shoot a couple more. Feels good. A couple more."

When Bill was a seventh grader, his parents agreed to let him stay with relatives in Crystal City while they went to Florida. "It was simple," he later said. "I wanted to play basketball, so I told my parents I didn't want to go. They weren't encouraging about the game—my father did not see me play until I was an eighth grader—but that was okay. I found that basketball was a place where I could discover things about myself."

Encouraging or not, Bill's parents were supportive. With the help of the family handyman, Leonard "Alex" Maul, Sue Bradley installed a regulation basket and backboard on a metal pole in the backyard, and local pavers were hired to lay a blacktop court beneath it. Over time, the Bradley house became a sort of neighborhood recreation center, complete with a punching bag and pinball machine in the basement, and the floodlit basketball court outdoors where Bill and his friends would practice night and day, in any weather.

By eighth grade, Bill was six feet one inches tall, and the high school football/basketball coach, Arvel Popp (pronounced "Pope"), envisioned him as a future All-American football end. To the coach's dismay, however, Bill didn't want to play football, only basketball, and he approached the sport the way his mother had taught him to approach other activities: by practicing. Maybe he felt he needed to prove himself to his coach and to those who doubted his courage because he wasn't playing football, but by age fourteen he was self-motivated, and the practice schedule he set for himself for the next four years would become the stuff of legend. Borrowing the keys to the gym from Coach Popp, Bill practiced three and a half hours a day six days a week, and six hours straight on Sundays. He practiced alone and he practiced systematically. Working around the basket, he would shoot from a spot until he could make ten shots in a row, and these included left-handed hook shots, perhaps the most difficult shot in basketball. He wore weights in his sneakers to strengthen his legs. He dribbled around chairs, wearing a cardboard shield below his eyes so that he couldn't watch his dribble. From behind stacked chairs, he made jump shot after jump shot. He talked to himself, encouraged himself, forced himself to concentrate.

Years later, Bill told John McPhee that he would never forget something he learned from "Easy" Ed Macauley, a pro player whose basketball camp in St. Louis Bill attended every summer. Macauley said, "When you are not practicing, remember, someone somewhere is practicing, and when you meet him he will win."

Bill's hard work and self-discipline paid off. To the amazement of many, the banker's son made the high school varsity basketball team in his freshman year, averaging twenty points a game and demonstrating to his coach and others his true mettle. His style of play was pure, not flashy; unselfish, never hotdogging. He was as brilliant a passer as he was a shooter, and he brought out the best in his—at first—resentful older teammates. In four years as a Crystal City Hornet, Bill scored over three thousand points, leading by example, and won high school All-American honors his junior and senior years. Yet basketball wasn't his only achievement. He maintained honor grades, attended Sunday school at Grace Presbyterian, earned his Eagle badge as a Boy Scout, ran the student council, and was elected Missouri state student council president his senior year. By then averaging thirty-eight points a game, he was recruited by seventy-five colleges that wanted him

Crystal's Bradley Again Hits Above 30

By Bob Ruhl

As the final seconds ticked away last night, Elroe Wallace...

Crystal, Festus Clash In Game For 1st Place

15 seconds remaining in the extra period, Wallace again flipped a free toss through the net...
60-59 victory.

The victory...
Hank H...

Hornets Swamp Desloge; Edge Junior Billikens

Hornets Win Over Farmington,

Crystal City won it secutive basketball vict... ...nowering Farmington,
...ng at Crysta...
...nets led by...
...ssion but broke the game... in the second half.
...dley poured in 36 p...
...l scorers. Sa...
...ntinued hi...
...hitting...

Hornets Down Hillsboro, 90-65

Crystal Hornets Rank Third in St. Louis Area

BOX SC...

Hornets Beat Knights 90-46; Bradley Gets 36

Crystal City played a fine second half last night to defeat Farmington's basketball team 90-46 after leading at intermission by only eight points. Bill Bradley paced the Hornets to their 16th ...ight victory by tallying 36 ...nts.

...op scorers for the visiting ...ights, who trailed at the...
28, were Littles with...
...and Jolly at...
...ves and...
...nton...

Hornets Win 15th Straight ... In Tourney

...n be host ...ouse Springs ...s Friday evening.

C.C. Hornets Win Razor Edge S.L.U. Victory, 67-66

Hornets downed Flat River 78-45, with Bradley assisting in several of his teammates baskets.

The 6-5 senior now has close to a 30-point average for 68 games in his high school career. He has scored under 20 points in only nine games over the past two-and-a-half seasons.

St. Louis U. High boosted its mark to 10-1 by defeating a battling Ritenour team, 55-39. The Junior Bills led at the half, 30-13, but the Huskies outscored ...
...4, in the first five min... the third period and p...
within four points, 34-...
Louis then settled down ...
rapidly away.

Duchesne Theater...
Marquette held a 41-20... tage over Duchesne at t... but Duchesne put on a fur...

Test in S.L.U. Game Friday

Ho...

Hornets, De Soto Win; Herky, Fox, Northwest Cagers Lose

A collage of clippings from the Crystal City High School yearbook

to play basketball for them. After much soul-searching, he chose an Ivy League college, Princeton, turning down scholarship offers at big-name basketball schools and baffling critics who felt his playing talents would be wasted on relatively minor Ivy League competition.

BILL BRADLEY FLOURISHED AT Princeton—as a scholar and as an athlete. By his own admission he hadn't been much of a reader through high school. "Oh, sure, some of the children's classics, some of the Dr. Dolittle books, *The Deerslayer*, things like that," he recalled to a reporter later, "but nothing with much heft." Princeton changed all that. "Maybe my coming late to [reading] explains why it took, but, anyhow, it did. When the books came off the shelf, they fell off."

Bill read widely while at Princeton, finding his greatest satisfaction studying history, both European and American. In the early 1960s, when he was a student, the United States was undergoing a period of change. In a stirring inaugural address, the nation's new president, John F. Kennedy, had challenged Americans to "ask not what your country can do for you—ask what you can do for your country." Many people understood this as a call to help others. Some joined the president's new volunteer organization, the Peace Corps, to help people in underdeveloped countries. Others volunteered their services in America's inner cities, where poverty, crime, and illiteracy were rampant. Still others, inspired by the example of Martin Luther King, Jr., joined the civil rights movement to challenge segregationist laws in the deep South.

All of these activities, coupled with his reading in American history and his growing personal beliefs about helping others, had a profound impact on Bill. In the late spring of 1964, when he was working as an intern in Washington, D.C., for Pennsylvania governor William Scranton's presidential campaign, the United States Senate was debating a bill that, if it became law, would bar discrimination in voting, education, and public accommodation.

At Princeton, Bill led the Tigers to three consecutive Ivy League basketball championships, as well as to the NCAA Final Four.

During every free moment he had, Bill would rush to the Capitol to hear the debate in the Senate chamber. On the night of June 19, 1964, he was present when the Senate voted 73 to 27 in favor of the Civil Rights Act. He was twenty years old. He later told a reporter that he felt that "something really important happened in that room that day, that people's lives could change for the better because of it." It was also "the first moment it dawned on me that maybe someday I might like to be in the Senate."

For the time being, however, he was too young and too busy winning basketball games for Princeton. At six feet five, he was only the third tallest man on the team, but he was the best player ever to have played in the Ivy League, and many considered him the best amateur player in the history of basketball. He led the Princeton Tigers to three consecutive Ivy League titles but, more impressive, demonstrated that an Ivy team could hold its own against bigger basketball powerhouses and even win. For example, Princeton was considered the lowliest of underdogs in the 1965 eastern finals against Providence College, which had lost only one game all season. But Bill scored 41 points, he and his teammates played tight defense, and Princeton won the game 109–69, the first Ivy League team in twenty years to win an eastern championship. Later, in the National Collegiate Athletic Association semifinals, unranked Princeton lost to top-ranked Michigan, 93–76. But in the consolation game against Wichita State—the last of Bill's college career—Princeton won 118–82, and Bill scored 58 points, breaking Oscar Robertson's tournament scoring record of 56 points and earning honors as the tournament's most valuable player.

At the end of his Princeton career, Bill was the third highest scorer in the history of college basketball, with 2,503 points. He won the 1965 Sullivan Award as the nation's outstanding amateur athlete, and a Rhodes scholarship to Oxford University in England, one of thirty-two given every year to some of the best scholar athletes in America.

A year earlier, Bill had captained the United States Olympic Basketball Team to a gold medal–winning victory over the Soviets in Tokyo. Now many sports pundits assumed he would forsake Oxford and cash in on his basketball fame by turning pro. The New York Knickerbockers even made him their first-round choice in the annual player draft. But Bill had other plans. In the fall of 1965, he enrolled as a student at Oxford's Worcester College, declaring politics, philosophy, and economics as his major, or, as the British call it, P P & E.

Bill's basketball achievements at Princeton had brought him an unwanted amount of public attention. Organizations sought him out for speaking engagements, sportswriters seemed always to be pestering for interviews, and even *The New Yorker* magazine, which rarely covers sports celebrities, ran a profile on him by John McPhee that later became the basis for a book. At Oxford, the attention slackened. Though he still received as many as fifty letters a week from friends, well-wishers, and admirers, by and large he was treated as just another student, which suited Bill fine. Besides reading, writing papers, and attending lectures for his courses, he read on his own the novels of such great European writers as Leo Tolstoy, Fyodor Dostoyevski, Thomas Mann, and Albert Camus. His biggest discovery, he said later, was Joseph Conrad, the Polish-English writer whose novels include *Heart of Darkness, Victory*, and *Lord Jim*. "[Conrad's] view of society as a fragile superstructure of orderliness over a massive network of darker human impulses really stopped me," Bill said. "His drifters, the chronic floaters, made me think about myself, made me see how important the stop-drift mechanisms are."

Not that Bill had to worry about his life drifting. What little free time he could manage away from his studies he spent playing soccer, running, wrestling—and playing basketball. Though he thought he had retired from the sport when he came to Oxford, he found he could not shake his love of playing. After only a few months he was practicing a few hours a day at a U.S. military base gym several miles from Oxford, and he accepted the invitation from an Italian basketball team, Simmenthal, to play for them twice a month, in Milan, in European cup competition.

For a while, Bill thought he might go to law school after Oxford. But one night in his second year, as he was shooting baskets alone in the newly constructed Oxford indoor gym, the

Bill at Oxford University, 1966. Oxford's arches were not designed for someone 6'5".

first ever in its eight-hundred-year history, he realized that he wanted to play professional basketball "to test myself against the best." That spring, he flew to New York and signed a four-year contract with the New York Knickerbockers for the then-unheard-of sum of five hundred thousand dollars.

Sportswriters heralded his signing as the dawn of a new age for pro basketball. Bill joined the Knicks, as *New York Times* columnist Robert Lipsyte wrote, "on the wings of hype." For his part, Bill had mixed feelings about accepting money to play a game he loved. "If I had to, I would have played for nothing," he said. As it was, he chose to make no commercial endorsements as a player, a decision that probably cost him hundreds of thousands of dollars over the length of his career. He also avoided the fancy clothes, cars, and houses typically purchased by pro players, instead choosing to live simply and frugally. He drove an old Volkswagen, rented a small apartment on Eighth Avenue in Manhattan, and dressed in black shoes and well-worn two-piece suits. His Knicks teammates forever kidded him about his lackluster garb. "Bradley never has to worry about being mugged," said one, "because he dresses as if he's already *been* mugged." "Dollar Bill" became his nickname on the Knicks, owing to his seeming thriftiness.

By his own estimation, Bill's first year in the pros was a disappointment. He averaged only eight points a game and often appeared to be outplayed by his quicker, more experienced opponents. Of course, his two-year layoff from tough competition while at Oxford was a factor in his poor play, but Bill would not make excuses for himself. In silence, he suffered the boos and jeers of the Knicks crowds, and when the season ended he decided to take drastic measures to improve his game. He joined the Baker League, a high-caliber summer basketball league in Philadelphia that combined outstanding street players with some of the biggest names in the NBA. Playing for Jimmy Bates's B-Bar, Bill sharpened all facets of his game, and when he wasn't playing he was back in New York, practicing alone.

Although his first year as a pro player for the New York Knicks was disappointing, Bill later helped lead the Knicks to two NBA championships. He was elected to the Basketball Hall of Fame during his first year of eligibility, in 1982.

Once again, his determination paid off. In his next season as a Knick, he proved he was a pro by scoring more than 1,000 points, collecting more than 300 rebounds and 300 assists, and averaging 12.4 points a game. With starting teams that included Dave DeBusschere and Bill at forward, Willis Reed at center, and Walt Frazier, Dick Barnett, and later Earl Monroe at guard, the Knicks went on to win NBA championships in 1970 and 1973. Bill became a solid, consistent pro player, and the boos that greeted him his first year in the league turned to cheers.

BILL BRADLEY KNEW THAT his career as a basketball player would someday be over, and that he would have to decide what to do with the rest of his life. He had thought about entering law or business, but when he honestly weighed his options, he realized that, more than anything, he wanted to enter politics.

Why politics?

As a boy in Missouri he had watched relatives run for county offices, and politics was often discussed at dinner. "I was always aware of politics as a profession, as something that you could *do*," he once said. At Oxford, he had admired the English approach to public service—as something that you *studied* for. That approach jibed with his approach to basketball. And his religious beliefs since boyhood told him "it's one's job to serve, one's calling. My view of politics derives from that," he said.

And so Bill used basketball as a means to prepare for a likely political future. Pro basketball teams' schedules keep them criss-crossing the country, and at every stop the Knicks made, Bill went around "looking at America." He talked to people his age who were just starting to run for political office "to see how they were going about it." He made notes on the conversations he had with average Americans in airports, diners, restaurants, and coffee shops. He visited museums, markets, Indian reservations, factories. And he read books on banking, taxation, prison reform, oil—issues he wanted to tackle if he ever entered politics.

Between seasons, Bill used his free time to travel abroad. He went to such countries as India, China, Japan, Afghanistan, Turkey, and the Soviet Union to learn about other peoples and governments. In the Soviet Union and Eastern Europe he made friends with whom he is still in contact. In India he would eventually meet Mother Teresa, whose own dedication to service made a lasting impression on him.

At home, he fell in love with Ernestine Schlant, a professor of German language and literature who lived in his building and had

Bill and his wife, Ernestine, watching news shows, waiting for the polls to close in the 1978 New Jersey Democratic primary. Bill won the primary, and later the general election, to become, at age thirty-five, the youngest member of the United States Senate.

a young daughter, Stephanie, by a previous marriage. Bill and Ernestine were married in 1974. A year later, the notes he had been keeping about his experience as a pro basketball player became a book, *Life on the Run*. Then, in 1976, the Bradleys had a daughter of their own, Theresa Anne, and Bill knew, approaching his tenth year in the pros, that it was time to call it quits and turn to politics. By then, he and his family had moved to a comfortable eight-room house in Denville, New Jersey, which they now called home.

In 1977, Bill retired from the Knicks, and in the spring of 1978, he announced his candidacy for the United States Senate. Many people wondered whether an ex-jock had what it took to be a senator, but Bill's intelligence and tenacity silenced those who felt he was only cashing in on his fame. Campaigning eighteen hours a day on the issues of tax relief, energy development, and urban improvement, he easily defeated his conservative Republican opponent, Jeffrey K. Bell. In doing so, he became, at thirty-five, the youngest member of the Senate, and, as he later joked, the only senator who could sink a foul shot. The quiet, self-motivated boy from Crystal City had come a long way, but he would discover that the traits that had served him so well in basketball—hard work, discipline, a passionate dedication to excellence—would now serve him well in the Senate.

3

ON BEING A UNITED STATES SENATOR

THE UNITED STATES CONGRESS, which performs its duties in the Capitol building in Washington, D.C., is composed of two bodies, the Senate and the House of Representatives. Each body has specific duties as defined by the U.S. Constitution, yet both share a common purpose: to make laws. Most laws are proposed in either house in the form of bills—also called legislation. A majority of each house must vote for a bill before it is sent to the president to be signed into law.

The House of Representatives is composed of 435 members, often called congressmen, each elected for a two-year term from a separate district in one of the fifty states.* The Senate is composed of 100 members, two from each state, and each elected for a six-

---

* Six states—Alaska, Delaware, North Dakota, South Dakota, Vermont, and Wyoming—each have only one representative, who represents the entire state.

The Capitol building, Washington, D.C. The United States Senate meets in the right-hand wing of the building. When the Senate is in session, the American flag flies atop the Senate chamber's roof.

year term. Because a senator represents an entire state and not just a single district, he is responsible to more people or *constituents* than a congressman is. In addition, the Senate alone has the power to advise and consent—that is, to vote on foreign treaties and on appointments by the president for government posts (many senators find themselves serving on committees that interview nominees for such positions). Also, unlike the House of Representatives, which sets time restraints on how long it will consider a bill, the Senate has a rule allowing unlimited debate on any legislation. All this means that effective senators must have a number of special talents. They must care about the people in their entire state enough to represent them well. They must be good legislators, able to push bills through into laws. They must be able to ask tough questions of presidential appointees. And they must be able to debate.

WHEN FRESHMAN SENATOR BILL Bradley arrived in Washington in January 1979, he knew he had his work cut out for him. For one

Interior, the United States Senate

SEATING ARRANGEMENT IN THE SENATE CHAMBER

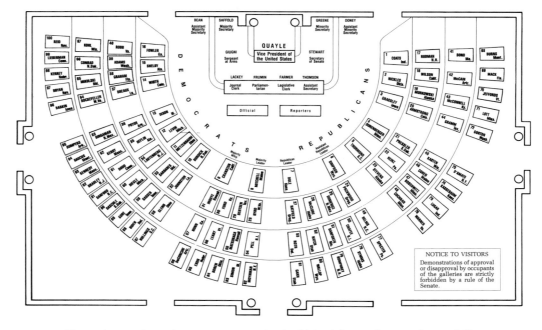

Floor plan and seating arrangement in the United States Senate during Bill's second term

thing, he had to learn the Senate rules and procedures for getting legislation passed. For another, he had to have a sound grasp of all the issues he would confront as a senator, particularly those relating to the Senate committees he'd serve on. For a third, he had to get to know the 99 other senators he would work with so he'd know who to count on when he needed support for his own legislation.

Bill knew something else as well: that he'd have to learn to speak and debate better if he was going to be listened to and respected by his Senate colleagues. "After all," he said, "I spent ten years in an essentially nonverbal profession [basketball]. Now I'm in a profession where the only thing that's important is what I say."

Like any newly elected lawmaker, Bill began his work in the Senate by hiring a staff to help him fulfill his senatorial duties. Part of that staff was hired to perform housekeeping and service tasks—answering the telephones, typing, scheduling, greeting visitors, handling mail, dealing with the media, and solving constituents' problems. The other part, the legislative staff, was hired to help Bill fulfill his legislative duties. He says, "I tried to put together a legislative staff that included people both from inside and outside Washington, and that combined experience and creativity, freshness and wisdom. I also knew that I had never been in a legislative body and that it was very important to get people who understood the legislative process." Over Bill's two terms as a senator, staffers have come and gone, but the total number has remained a near-constant thirty-six. Of those, five are Bill's chief legislative assistants, with the rest fulfilling other necessary duties.

One of a senator's rudest shocks upon election to the Senate is the sheer number of bills that must be dealt with each year. In 1989, for example, 7,390 bills were introduced in Congress, and 1990 brought 6,963 more. To handle this legislative avalanche, both houses of Congress assign bills to committees that decide which should be voted on by their full legislative body. There are currently twenty-two standing committees in the House of Representatives, and sixteen standing committees in the Senate, as well as two joint committees comprised of senators and House members. Each committee has its own special area of jurisdiction, and usually Senate and House members serve on several of them. In addition, there are five select and special committees of the House, and four select and special committees of the Senate, each of which performs either investigative or monitoring duties, rather than recommending legislation.

As President Woodrow Wilson once wrote, "Congressional government is committee government," and Bill Bradley understood this fact as well as any senator. He knew freshmen are assigned to committees by Senate leaders and committee chairmen, and he visited potentially helpful senior senators to indicate his assignment preferences: Finance and Energy. Why these two? Bill says, "When I made my choices I considered the committees that I thought would give me the best opportunity to pursue New Jersey's interests and the future interests of our nation. In addition, I had done some work for the New Jersey Department of Energy and I have always had a strong interest in the tax system, so the Finance and Energy committees seemed right for my interests and experience."

Fortunately, he won those two assignments, and, with the same zeal that he once applied to practicing basketball, he set about learning everything he could about his committee work and about Senate business in general. His family remained in New Jersey. He bought a small house in Washington. Arriving on Capitol Hill early every morning, he would work all day in the Senate and in his office in the Dirksen Senate Office Building, not returning to his house until after midnight. In his free time he studied the speeches of Woodrow Wilson and other great American orators to develop his speech-making skills. And whenever he could, he volunteered to preside over the Senate—that is, to serve as its moderator, making sure that sessions ran smoothly and according

Bill in his office, in the Hart Senate Office Building

to Senate rules. Few senators enjoy this task, but Bill found it to be the perfect way to master the intricate rules and procedures that govern the Senate's activity. In addition, he spent hours at a time interviewing the Senate parliamentarian—the resident expert on Senate rules—to further understand when and how to use them. Again his diligent preparation paid off. For presiding over the body for one hundred hours in his first year, Bill received from Vice President Walter Mondale the Golden Gavel Award. And when he supported his first bill in the Senate—a move to keep the aircraft carrier U.S.S. *Saratoga* in the Philadelphia Naval Yard for refurbishment and thereby bring billions of dollars in jobs and income to Delaware, Pennsylvania, and New Jersey—he used his improved speaking skills and recently learned understanding of the rules to defeat those senators who wanted the ship moved elsewhere and thus got the bill passed.

According to many historians, the old Senate gavel was used by the nation's first vice president, John Adams, to call the first Senate session to order in New York City in 1789. When the ivory gavel began to splinter in 1947, silver disks were added to reinforce it. In 1954 it was retired, and a new ivory gavel, presented as a gift from the government of India, replaced it.

Bill was discovering that a major part of a senator's job consists of three things: what he calls substance, procedure, and personality.

"First," he says, "you have to know what you're talking about—meaning that you have to master the substance of your committees. If you don't know what you're talking about, nobody listens. If you don't have control of the facts, you can't convince anybody to adopt your position.

"Second, you have to know Senate procedure. I've seen a lot of senators with great ideas who can't move the ideas through Congress because they don't understand the procedure. I've seen senators cut down on the Senate floor either because they hadn't followed procedure, or because they weren't clever enough to dodge an attack with a procedural effort.

"As far as personality goes, you've got to understand who the other senators are. You've got to understand how to move them to do what you want them to do—understand their personalities, their interests, who you want to speak for you, and who you want to speak against you."

Late one night, after he had been in the Senate about four months, Bill was in the Democratic cloakroom, which is right off the Senate floor. (There is also a nearby Republican cloakroom.) With their big leather couches and telephones for members' use, these two chambers serve senators as both lounges and information hubs. Now, as Bill looked around his party's cloakroom, he saw two senators talking, a third telling a joke, a fourth sitting quietly, and a fifth pacing the floor. He suddenly realized that the place wasn't a lot different from the Knicks' locker room. It was an important insight for him. "The core of both experiences," he said later, "is about getting people with disparate backgrounds and different personal agendas to agree on a common goal and work toward it. And I think that realization—which I got from sport—made me feel comfortable rather quickly as a senator."

Bill also credits his Energy Committee chairman, Henry "Scoop" Jackson of Washington, and his Finance Committee chairman, Russell Long of Louisiana, for being his unsuspecting mentors during his first term. "Watching them conduct Senate business was an education," Bill says, "because each of them approached it quite differently. Scoop Jackson was a planner: define the issue, lay things out, build a massive record in support of your position, go to the battle on the floor, don't worry about tricks, just marshal your forces and run over your opponent. Russell Long, on the other hand, was much more spontaneous, much more the virtuoso, much more the person who used surprise, procedure, intimidation, and all the rest to make things move. And, though you thought he was in control of things in committee and on the floor, you weren't quite sure, because he was always bringing bills back to committee and throwing things into them, basically to confuse you so that only he knew what was going to happen.

"Russell's wisdom and ability constantly amazed me. Both he

Russell Long of Louisiana   Henry "Scoop" Jackson of Washington

and Scoop provided me with models for being a senator that were quite different, and, in their own ways, equally effective."

Bill developed an approach to being a senator that now reflects his appreciation of both Long's and Jackson's legislative styles. Like Long, he tends to be secretive about new issues he is studying, lest any opposition try to undermine his legislative efforts before they get started. He won't even tell reporters about his casual reading. He does that, says one of his staffers, "because he doesn't want people thinking that the book he's reading contains the next issue that he'll tackle. It's hard to study an issue with the media watching your every move. So Bill stays quiet about his research until he's ready to unveil his legislative plan."

Like Henry Jackson, Bill relies on fact to build a massive record of information in support of his legislative position. "Bill Bradley has always been a person who makes a decision based on facts," his 1978 campaign manager and close political advisor Susan Thomases says. This is where his legislative staff helps him. "I only have twenty-four hours in a day," Bill says, "and I have an enormous plate of material—many, many things to do. So I divide my legislative staff, delegate some authority to them in specific areas, and supervise them rather rigorously. Ultimately, nothing big happens unless it goes through me—I'm either a bottleneck or a funnel or a source of changes. But basically my staff responds to me."

Through a combination of hard work, research, study, persistence, patience, and caring, Bill began to see his legislative efforts bear fruit. President Carter's 1979 Synthetic Fuels Act, for example, contained three titles that Bill championed: refilling America's Strategic Petroleum Reserves, or SPRO; authorizing $83 million to help develop garbage-to-energy systems, and authorizing $10 million to encourage private firms to increase home energy efficiency without cost to the homeowner. In education, Bill got legislation passed to provide money for elementary and secondary school programs for gifted and talented students. He also sponsored the Geography Awareness Resolution, which challenges elementary schools to develop class geography projects. It led him to start the annual Geography Bee in New Jersey, an event that, with the support of the National Geographic Society, went national in 1989. He was also one of the chief Senate sponsors of Superfund legislation, which now provides money for cleaning up toxic dumps. And when medical waste began washing up along the Eastern shoreline, Bill helped push through the Medical Waste Tracking Act, which provides penalties for polluters, including jail terms.

By doing his homework, knowing procedures, and getting useful legislation passed, Bill proved to his Senate colleagues that he was a workhorse, not a showhorse. Toward the end of his second year, political writer Jack Anderson categorized Bill as "Most Respected," "Most Effective," and "the Senate's Resident Brain Trust." "He's the most likely to twinkle in the Senate," Anderson wrote.

"I just want to be the best senator I can be," Bill said.

By far, Bill's biggest legislative triumph in his first two terms as senator was tax reform. In order for the federal government to fund its programs, including defense, education, space exploration,

and many others, it levies a tax on individual and corporate earnings, or income. Since the inception of the income tax in 1913,
special-interest groups had successfully gotten Congress to add
"loopholes" to the tax laws, allowing business, industry, and some
individuals to deduct certain expenses from their taxable income,
thereby reducing their tax bills. In some cases, because they had
so many deductions, corporations weren't paying any income taxes
at all!

To many, including Bill Bradley, this didn't seem fair. As early
as 1980, he began proposing the idea of an income tax that freed
poor people from paying any tax at all and that closed the loopholes
and lowered the tax rates for everyone else.

At first, the plan was met with amused derision. The common
view was that any tax reform bill put before Congress would be
chopped to pieces by special interest groups demanding that their
loopholes be left in place. Bill persisted. He talked to other senators
about tax reform, gave speeches on the subject. He even wrote a
book called *The Fair Tax* to show how his plan would work. Yet
few would rally around Bill's idea.

Then, in 1984, President Ronald Reagan said that *he* favored
tax reform and would make it one of the goals of his second term.
Suddenly, in a Republican president, Bill had an unexpected ally.
He spent the next two years trying to rally support for tax reform,
and in the fall of 1986, after months of Senate and House debate,
he had the supreme satisfaction of seeing what was essentially *his*
idea made into law.

The Tax Reform Act of 1986 was one of the most sweeping
pieces of legislation passed in decades. It forever established Bill
Bradley as a major force in the U.S. Senate. People began urging
him to run for president in 1988, but Bill declined, saying it wasn't
his time. Instead, from tax reform he moved to the complicated
issue of Third World debt. He proposed that poor countries should
be excused from repaying part of the billions of dollars in loans
they owe to American and European banks. Not surprisingly, bank

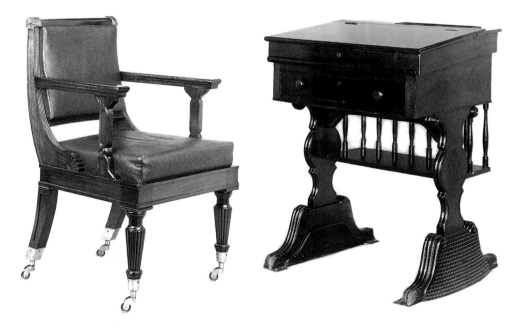

A Senate desk and chair. Forty of the desks date back to 1819. All desks include an inkwell and sand shaker for blotting ink. It is a Senate tradition for retiring senators to carve their name inside their desk drawer.

leaders didn't like Bill's proposal, but when the Reagan administration revealed its solution for dealing with the problem, it closely resembled Bill's plan.

IN THE SENATE CHAMBER, in the drawers of its cherrywood desks, Bill Bradley has seen the handiwork of past senators who, with penknives or pocket knives, have carved their names in the drawers' fragrant wood. Names such as Robert LaFollette, Robert Taft, J. William Fulbright, John F. Kennedy, Lyndon Johnson, Harry Truman, and Margaret Chase Smith remind Bill that Senate history is human history, and that we each have our moment in time, and then that time passes.

His own time would someday pass, he knew, but not yet. There was still work he wanted to do. And the determination to do it.

4

HOW A BILL
BECOMES A LAW

As BILL BRADLEY CAN tell you, the chief responsibility of senators and representatives is making laws, and lawmaking can begin in several ways. Usually a prospective law is introduced to either or both houses in the form of a bill. In the House of Representatives, introducing a bill is as simple as dropping a copy of it into a hopper provided for the purpose in the House chamber. In the Senate, the rules state that a member shall introduce the bill three times, during three separate legislative sessions, though, in fact, all a senator need do for the first two introductions, or readings, is hand the bill to the Senate clerks at the presiding officer's desk. The bill can then be referred to an appropriate committee.

Usually senators introduce a bill from the Senate floor, and most include remarks for the record about why they feel the bill is necessary. They also usually ask that the bill appear as part of the day's business in the *Congressional Record*, the daily printed account of proceedings in the House and Senate.

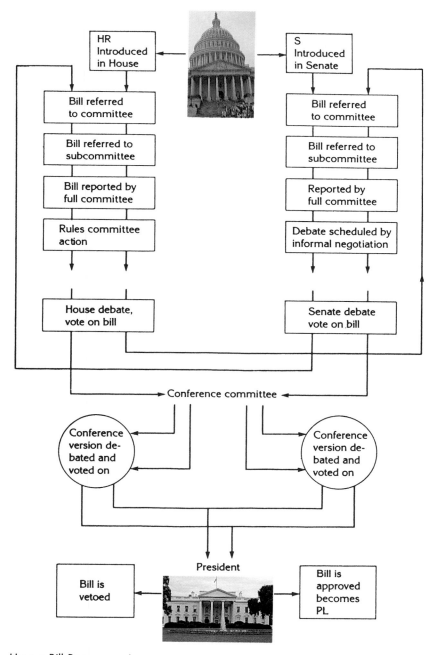

How a Bill Becomes a Law
As this diagram shows, the process by which a bill becomes public law (PL) is slow and complex.

Once a bill is introduced, it is given a sequential number, beginning with "S." if it originates in the Senate and with "H.R." if it originates in the House of Representatives. Then it is catalogued, computerized, and assigned to a standing committee. In the House of Representatives, such assignments are implemented by a leader called the Speaker of the House; in the Senate, by the presiding officer.

Most committees are comprised of smaller subcommittees that are often assigned the task of studying a bill and reporting their findings to the full committee. They perform their work by holding hearings where invited witnesses speak for or against the bill, and then they review the bill section by section, word by word, and recommend in their written report whether or not it should be adopted. A full committee can either accept or reject a subcommittee's report, or it can change the report or throw it out and write a new one. Bills that are "marked up"—reviewed, changed where necessary, and approved by a majority of the full committee—are returned to the House or Senate for a vote by the full membership. Bills that don't survive committee markup most often die. In this way, committees serve as filters for the full House or Senate, allowing only those bills they approve to pass through for further consideration.

In the House, a bill that has been favorably reported out of its committee goes to the Rules committee, which determines how long the bill will be debated by the full membership before a vote is taken on it. In the Senate, where debate is unlimited, members can, and often do, unanimously agree to limit debate so a bill can be moved to a vote more quickly. If a controversial bill is given unlimited debate, that debate can be halted by three-fifths of the Senators voting for "cloture," or closing of debate.

Bills presented before the full House or Senate can be amended (changed), with each amendment accepted or rejected by majority vote. Once a bill has gone through this process of amendment and debate, it is reintroduced, or "read," for a third time and voted

Congressional Record

United States of America

PROCEEDINGS AND DEBATES OF THE 101st CONGRESS, SECOND SESSION

| *Vol. 136* | WASHINGTON, TUESDAY, JUNE 19, 1990 | *No. 78* |

Senate

(Legislative day of Monday, June 11, 1990)

The Senate met at 9:30 a.m., on the expiration of the recess, and was called to order by the Honorable HARRY REID, a Senator from the State of Nevada.

PRAYER

The Chaplain, the Reverend Richard C. Halverson, D.D., offered the following prayer:

Let us pray:

* * * *but with God all things are possible.*—Matthew 19:26.

Almighty God, to whom belongs all power and all wisdom, manifest Thyself in this place that all may know that Thou art present and relevant. Certainly anything that is doable this powerful body can do. But despite all its power, some issues are beyond human resolution and require divine remedy. As the Senate labors under internal as well as external pressures, confronting not only the issues from without but the struggle of conscience, courage, and confidence from within, as stubborn problems refuse solution and an impending election pervades the atmosphere, help Your servants to learn to depend upon the God of the impossible as they try to do everything that is possible.

In the name of Jesus for whom nothing is impossible. Amen.

APPOINTMENT OF ACTING PRESIDENT PRO TEMPORE

The PRESIDING OFFICER. The clerk will please read a communication to the Senate from the President pro tempore [Mr. BYRD].

The legislative clerk read the following letter:

U.S. SENATE,
PRESIDENT PRO TEMPORE,
Washington, DC, June 19, 1990.
To the Senate:

Under the provisions of rule I, section 3, of the Standing Rules of the Senate, I hereby appoint the Honorable HARRY REID, a Senator from the State of Nevada, to perform the duties of the Chair.

ROBERT C. BYRD,
President pro tempore.

Mr. REID thereupon assumed the chair as Acting President pro tempore.

RECOGNITION OF THE MAJORITY LEADER

The ACTING PRESIDENT pro tempore. Under the standing order, the majority leader is now recognized.

THE JOURNAL

Mr. MITCHELL. Mr. President, I ask unanimous consent that the Journal of the proceedings be approved to date.

The ACTING PRESIDENT pro tempore. Without objection, it is so ordered.

SCHEDULE

Mr. MITCHELL. Mr. President, following the time for the two leaders, there will be a period for morning business not to extend beyond 10 a.m., with Senators permitted to speak therein for up to 5 minutes each.

At 10 this morning, the Senate will resume consideration of S. 566, the affordable housing bill, with amendment No. 2024 the pending business.

The yeas and nays have been ordered on this amendment, so my colleagues should be aware that there is the possibility of a rollcall vote this morning relative to that amendment.

Other votes are likely today with respect to the housing bill. Between the hours of 12:30 p.m. and 2:15 p.m., the Senate will stand in recess to accommodate the party conference luncheons.

RESERVATION OF LEADER TIME

Mr. MITCHELL. Mr. President, I reserve the remainder of my leader time and reserve all the leader time of the distinguished Republican leader.

The ACTING PRESIDENT pro tempore. Without objection, the time of the two leaders is reserved.

MORNING BUSINESS

The ACTING PRESIDENT pro tempore. Under the previous order, there will now be a period for the transaction of morning business to extend to the hour of 10 a.m., with Senators permitted to speak therein for up to 5 minutes each.

Mr. MITCHELL. Mr. President, I suggest the absence of a quorum.

The ACTING PRESIDENT pro tempore. The clerk will call the roll.

The legislation clerk proceeded to call the roll.

Mr. GORE. Mr. President, I ask unanimous consent that the order for the quorum call be rescinded.

The ACTING PRESIDENT pro tempore. Without objection, it is so ordered. The Senator is recognized to speak in morning business.

REVERSAL OF ADMINISTRATION ENVIRONMENTAL POLICY

Mr. GORE. Mr. President, I rise to discuss two issues related to the global environment. On Friday afternoon, after we had finished our business for the week here and when many Senators were on their way to their home States, at the end of that day the administration quietly announced, in the form of a press release from John Sununu, that it was suddenly reversing its policy on the protection of the stratospheric ozone layer and was now prepared to join in a previously agreed measure to supply some funding for a pool of money to assist some of the poorest nations in the world to develop and use substitutes for the chemicals that are now implicated in the destruction of the Earth's protective ozone shield.

The *Congressional Record* is the daily printed account of proceedings in the Senate and House of Representatives.

on. In either house a bill needs only a simple majority to pass. (Treaties with foreign governments, which are ratified, or passed, by the Senate alone require at least a two-thirds affirmative vote.) The bill is then sent to the other house, where it goes through the same committee process leading to debate, amendment, and approval or disapproval by the full body. If a bill approved in one house is not approved in the other, it usually dies. If a bill is approved in one house, but changed and then approved in the other, the bill goes before a conference committee to iron out the differences.

Conference committees are comprised of appointed representatives of both houses. These can be either elected senators and congressmen or staff people familiar with the given piece of legislation. Since Congress works on the two-party system—meaning its members ally themselves with either the Democratic or Republican party—the party with the most members always has more representation on any committee, including conferences. For example, if the Democrats hold the majority in Congress, a typical conference committee might be comprised of four Democrats and three Republicans each from the House and the Senate.

If differences are ironed out in conference committee, the compromise version of the bill, voted through in conference, goes to the House and the Senate for final passage. If it is passed by a majority of both houses in its entirety, the bill is "enrolled"—printed on parchment—and signed by the Speaker of the House and the vice president of the United States acting in his role as president of the Senate. It is then hand-delivered by messenger to the White House for action by the president of the United States.

The Constitution allows the president ten days to make one of the following choices: 1) He can sign the bill into law; 2) He can choose not to sign the bill, causing it, after ten days, to become law automatically; 3) He can veto the bill—meaning he can say no to it, sending it back to Congress with his objections to it; 4) If Congress adjourns (ends its session) for the year before ten days are up, the president can choose not to sign the bill and it thereby automatically fails to become law. This is called a "pocket veto."

A vetoed bill dies unless it receives a two-thirds vote of both houses of Congress. This is known as overriding the presidential veto. The bill automatically becomes law. The president has no further opportunity to approve or reject it.

Senators and congressmen know when they introduce a bill in the Senate or the House that its chances of being made into law can be slim. Of the 6,900-plus bills introduced in 1990, only several hundred found their way into law. Often the finished product, packed as it is with amendments and changes, scarcely resembles the original bill. Also, the process by which the bill becomes law can seem ponderously slow, taking months or even years to complete.

"As a legislator you have to have patience," Bill Bradley says. "You have to be committed to something over a period of years if you're going to make it happen. You have to convince a majority of both houses *and* get the president's signature on the bill. It's much more a team atmosphere than if you're a decision-maker in the private sector or executive branch. You have to really care about an issue. When you begin you don't know whether you'll succeed or not. You begin because of what's inside you and what compels you to take that action."

In the winter of 1988, Bill Bradley began research on an issue he cared deeply about: students as athletes. His commitment to the issue would embark him on a legislative journey that would not end for two and a half years. All his knowledge of substance, procedure, and personality would be brought to bear on the issue. But the result, he felt, was well worth the energy and the effort.

5

THE BIRTH OF A LAW: PART I

ONE DAY IN FEBRUARY 1988, Bill Bradley received a visitor in his office in the Hart Senate Office Building. Congressman Ed Towns had walked from his office in the Longworth Building to discuss with Bill his idea for what he felt was an important piece of legislation.

The two men sat on green couches at one end of the office, and Towns asked Bill if he had had a chance to review the proposal for legislation that Towns had sent over a few weeks earlier. Bill said he had. It seemed that for the past two years, Towns and some of his staff had been doing research about the college graduation rates of student athletes compared to those of college students who don't play organized sports. Towns's research showed that, at many colleges, athletes were playing four years of sports but not graduating because they hadn't passed enough courses for a degree. Colleges were using kids as athletes—giving them schol-

Congressman Edolphus "Ed" Towns, from Bedford-Stuyvesant, New York's
11th District, in his Capitol office in the Longworth House Office Building

arships and other blandishments—but were not requiring them
to attend classes and study. The result: at the end of their college
careers many student athletes had nothing to show for their
efforts—no degree, no job prospects, no future. And the colleges,
having gotten all they could from these kids, just seemed to toss
them aside.

Furthermore, Towns's research showed that many coaches and
recruiters enticed kids into playing for their college or university
by claiming it would improve the kids' chances of making it to
the pros.

From his own athletic experience, Bill knew how empty those
claims could be. In 1987, for example, 12,000 young men played
college basketball, but of that number only 161 were drafted into
the National Basketball Association. That's 1 player out of every
75. (The overall average in all the major sports is fewer than 1
out of 100.) If the other 11,800-plus players had squandered their
academic careers thinking that they, too, would make the NBA,
then they had been tragically misguided.

And it wasn't just basketball. Bill knew the problem existed in football, too, and to a lesser degree in other major sports, such as baseball and track.

Towns said that when you considered the money that colleges and universities made from their athletic programs—as much as $50 billion a year, according to one estimate—it was easy to understand how many of them could forget their educational mission. Meanwhile, many decent high school athletes—especially those who come from disadvantaged minority backgrounds—tend not to think about their graduation chances. Instead they mainly think about making it to the pros. Such kids, dreaming of fame and riches, tend not to make rational choices of colleges. They usually end up choosing wrongly and wasting their educations.

"So," said Towns, getting down to business, "the idea I sent over is something I think we could develop together into legislation. I'm wondering if you would agree to carry it on the Senate side. I'm not sure what to call it yet. Maybe you and your staff will have some ideas."

Towns's idea was brilliantly simple. Every year, colleges and universities that receive money from the federal government and award athletic scholarships would be required by the legislation to submit information about the graduation rates of their student athletes to the secretary of education in Washington. The college or university would then be required to provide that same information to a potential student athlete being offered financial aid. In other words, before a high school athlete decided which college he would attend, he would be told his chances of graduating.

Bill immediately liked the idea for the legislation. It squared with his own concerns for athletically gifted kids. In fact, a month after this meeting he would see another of his bills, one calling for a national day of recognition for America's student athletes, sail through the Senate without debate. Also, since 1983, Bill and his office had sponsored an annual conference at Rutgers University for New Jersey's college-bound high school athletes. At the conference, coaches and pro athletes had an urgent message for the youngsters: make academics your top college priority. "You've got to be prepared to be the best you can be," Bill told an audience at one such conference. "Use the next couple of years to develop your academic capacities." Or, as guest basketball coach P. J. Carlesimo of Seton Hall put it: "Use your sport to get an education. Don't let your sport use you."

Bill Bradley felt that his position as a former Rhodes scholar and pro basketball star obliged him to give something back to America's athletic youth. Ultimately, he viewed Towns's legislation as a form of giving.

For Ed Towns, a black congressman from the predominantly black district of Bedford-Stuyvesant in Brooklyn, New York, the idea for the legislation originated from personal experience. In 1970, at Towns's urging, his parents, then living in North Carolina, took in a sixteen-year-old boy from Bedford-Stuyvesant who showed both academic and athletic promise. Says Towns: "He was an outstanding basketball player and an impressive person, but his father no longer lived with the family, and his mother was struggling to make ends meet. I knew he had a lot of basketball talent, and after he went to live with my parents he just continued to develop. By his senior year he found himself recruited by over a hundred colleges. One school's basketball team had a terrible graduation record, but the recruiter had somehow convinced my father and the boy it was the place he should go. When I found out, I called the boy and said, 'Look, I don't want to tell you what to do, but the institution you've chosen has a terrible graduation record. Its basketball players do not get the grades. If you ask me, I think you're making a mistake.'

"After that, he started looking at other colleges and he finally chose one from which he did graduate. And he played a little pro ball after college with the Knicks, the Suns, and the Bullets, who finally cut him. His name is Gregory Jackson. He often lectures youth groups now. He tells kids of his pro experience, 'One day

At Bill's annual Student Athlete Conference for New Jersey's athletically gifted high school students, speaker P. J. Carlesimo emphasizes academics over athletics.

Bill's former Knicks teammates often speak at the conference. Here, Bill with former Knick All-Pro guard Dick Barnett, now an education management director in New York City.

you're driving a Mercedes-Benz, the next day you're unemployed. You need something more than basketball. You need something in your head.' "

Towns concludes: "That whole college recruiting experience *really stuck with me*. If I had not been an informed person, Gregory would have wound up in that college with the terrible graduation record, and would have had *no chance* of getting a degree. It really bothered me that colleges don't release graduation information about their athletes. After that experience with Gregory I went to twenty-four athletes in Brooklyn who had gone to college but failed to obtain degrees and I asked each of them, 'If you had known that the university you attended only graduated a small percentage of athletes, would you have gone?' And they all said, 'No, I just didn't know.' Well, when I came to Congress in 1983 I resolved to do something about that."

Bill knew Towns was sitting on a good idea, but before he tried to move it into the United States Senate, he wanted to do what he did for any piece of prospective legislation: learn more about it. There are three major collegiate athletic governing bodies in America, of which the biggest and most influential, with 803 member colleges and universities, is the National Collegiate Athletic Association, or NCAA. (The other two are the NAIA, or National Association of Independent Athletics, and the NJCAA, or National Junior College Athletic Association.) Bill asked Towns if the NCAA had been contacted about the legislative idea, and Towns said his office had been in touch, but the NCAA had not been terribly responsive.

Bill felt that before they went any further they ought to bring the NCAA in and talk to them, and Towns agreed. The two legislators shook hands, both wondering where Towns's legislative idea would lead them.

A FEW DAYS AFTER the meeting, Bill's and Towns's staffs, working together, sent a letter to the NCAA, outlining their legislative

proposal. The NCAA's response was swift. They felt such legislation was unnecessary. They clearly did not like the notion of the
federal government telling colleges what to do, and they made no
bones about saying it. As one of Bill's staffers put it, "Basically,
the message we got from the NCAA was a great big raspberry."

Bill was unfazed. Let's call in their executive director, he said.

In late May, the newly appointed executive director of the
NCAA, Richard Schultz, flew with the association's lawyer to
Washington from headquarters in Mission, Kansas. For Schultz,
a tall, amiable, articulate man, the meeting with Bill and Towns
in Bill's office was an opportunity to launch himself in his new
position, and one of Bill's staff who was present that day remembers
him radiating integrity and goodwill. "Dick Schultz is a man of
real presence," the staffer said, "and it showed."

Also attending the meeting was the former basketball star for
the Washington Bullets, Tom McMillen, then a freshman congressman from central Maryland. A towering six feet ten and a
half inches tall, the silver-haired McMillen, too, was a former
Rhodes scholar who saw Towns's idea as a creative way of helping
student athletes make proper decisions.

The meeting went amiably enough. As Bill, Towns, and
McMillen listened, Schultz tried to explain why the legislation was
unnecessary. He said he felt sure his office could get the NCAA
to take action on supplying graduation data at their annual meeting
next January. Who needed federal legislation, was his message, if
the NCAA could address the issue itself?

Bill knew it wasn't as simple as that. The NCAA is divided
into two governing bodies, the Executive Director's Office and the
President's Commission, the latter body composed of thirty-five of
the association's college presidents. Already, member presidents
were making negative remarks in newspaper stories about the
proposed legislation, and Bill doubted they would take positive
action unless they saw a threat from Washington. So, to Schultz's
reassurances, Bill said in effect, That's all well and good, but we're

Congressman Tom McMillen

going to go ahead with the legislation anyway. Schultz flew back to Kansas knowing that Bill Bradley intended to hold the NCAA's feet to the fire.

Meanwhile, one of Bill's staffers, Bill Foster, had been contacting college and high school educators nationwide, soliciting their views on the need for the proposed legislation. Nearly every person Foster spoke to, including high school guidance counselors, principals, and coaches, said some type of legislation was needed to inform student athletes of their chances of graduating from a given college. Foster's reports, coupled with the possibility that the NCAA might take no action on its own, served only to strengthen Bill Bradley's belief in the legislation's necessity.

Bill Foster had also been working closely with the Senate Legislative Counsel to transform the Towns idea into a piece of legislation. Located in a suite of offices on the sixth floor of the Dirksen Senate Office Building, the Legislative Counsel is staffed by attorneys skilled at writing legal prose. By the time Schultz met with Bill, a draft of the legislation had been prepared on the

Senate side, and a similar draft had been prepared on the House side by its legislative writers. Few bills are ever passed in their original form, and many serve as the basis for Congress's focused study of an issue. Bill knew that the draft of his bill was rough and would doubtless be changed as more information was gathered. For now, though, all that was missing from the five-page bill was a name. What should it be called?

One night, about a week before the bill would be unveiled at a press conference, Foster and Nick Donatiello, Bill's twenty-eight–year-old press secretary, pondered the question of nomenclature. Both felt the bill was going to receive a lot of press attention and, therefore, should have a catchy name. They knew their boss viewed the bill as a disclosure act designed to help young athletes make decisions, and that he felt student athletes had the right to know a college's athlete graduation rate.

"We should call it something like the Right-to-Know Act," Bill Foster said.

"How about the *Student Athlete* Right-to-Know Act," Nick Donatiello suggested. Bill Bradley gave his approval to the name the next morning, as did Ed Towns and Tom McMillen. When the three men held their press conference in the House Education and Labor Committee room on June 13, 1988, that's what they called their bill.

The purpose of the press conference was simple: as sponsors of the legislation, Bill, Towns, and McMillen wanted to generate favorable publicity for it, and the easiest way to do that was to invite Washington-based reporters from newspapers around the country to hear their announcement and ask questions about the bill's necessity. Also, going public with the legislation served to keep pressure on the NCAA.

After the press conference, an aide for Ed Towns walked a copy of the bill into the House chamber and introduced it there by putting it in the clerk's hopper. Bill walked his copy into the Senate chamber, asked to be recognized by the presiding officer, and then

stated that he was introducing a bill that he requested be inserted in
the day's *Congressional Record*. At the end of the day, the presiding
officer assigned the bill to the Senate Labor and Human Resources
Committee, which has jurisdiction over education-related bills.
The bill was assigned a number, S.2498, by the secretary of the Senate's office, and printed overnight. By the next morning, thanks to
the press conference, small items about the bill's introduction appeared in newspapers throughout the country. Coupled with an editorial that Bill had written a few weeks earlier for the *New York
Times*, the newspaper stories helped to favorably publicize the Student Athlete Right-to-Know Act. A number of Bill's New Jersey
constituents wrote to him to voice their support for the measure.
Bill was pleased with the favorable response. The Student
Athlete Right-to-Know Act seemed properly launched.

Bill had another reason to feel pleased. Months earlier, when
his staff was still researching the legislation, Bill knew that if he
introduced the bill it would be assigned to Labor and Human
Resources. The question any legislator faces when his bill is assigned is, Who on the committee can I get to support it? Bill
decided to solicit the support of Labor and Human Resources'
chairman, Senator Edward M. Kennedy of Massachusetts. After
all, Bill reasoned, if a chairman supports a bill, won't a healthy
number of committee members and other senators follow his lead?

In five Senate terms Ted Kennedy had emerged from the
shadow of his martyred brothers, John and Robert, as a champion
of equal opportunities for all Americans, particularly educational
opportunities. Kennedy and Bill were friends with neighboring
desks in the Senate. They respected each other as lawmakers.

Kennedy liked the idea of disclosing graduation rates. He told
Bill he felt that *every* student ought to know his or her chances of
graduating from a college, not just athletes. Bill agreed, but both
men wondered what the chances were of passing an all-student
right-to-know act by itself. Each knew that a law called the Higher
Education Act, dealing with a variety of campus issues, was

Senator Edward M. Kennedy of Massachusetts became a staunch co-sponsor of the Student Athlete Right-to-Know Act.

scheduled for reauthorization (revision) in the next session of Congress, and that it would be the ideal vehicle for an all-student right-to-know provision. Bill and Kennedy concluded that a student *athlete* bill, if passed, could pave the way for a broader, more encompassing graduation rate disclosure act later on. As one of Bill's aides said, "Our legislation made a good starting point." So, in a private conversation, Kennedy told Bill that not only would he support Bill's legislation in committee, he'd like to be its cosponsor on the Senate floor. Bill and his staff were quietly pleased. Gaining Ted Kennedy as a cosponsor on the bill was a real plus. He was sure to keep it alive in committee. There was even optimistic talk in Bill's office about the bill being passed into law before the 100th Congress ended in November.

That optimism was short-lived. The Labor and Human Resources Committee was so swamped with other bills that there was no room on its schedule for S.2498. In addition, 1988 was a presidential election year, and senators from both parties, including Bill, found their regular schedules interrupted by whirlwind trips to different parts of the country to stump for presidential and congressional candidates. Time was running out for S.2498. A gathering of the House and Senate, called a congress, lasts two years, and in November 1988, the 100th Congress was drawing to a close. By congressional rules, a bill introduced during a congress but not made into law dies. This is what happened to S.2498. On October 27, it died. Bill Bradley was not upset. He'd reintroduce it into the Senate after the start of the 101st Congress in January. Besides, the NCAA would be meeting around then, and Bill was interested in seeing if it would take action to disclose student athlete graduation rates.

By THE END OF January 1989, the only action the NCAA had taken was a resolution by its President's Commission calling for the NCAA staff to draft its own plan for disclosing graduation rates. Bill was glad to see the NCAA doing *something*, but he nonetheless felt their action was too slight and too slow. On the morning of March 15, he reintroduced the Student Athlete Right-to-Know Act in the United States Senate. On that same morning, Ed Towns reintroduced the bill in the House.

The bill, now known as S.580, was slightly different from the original. Bill and his staff had tightened the language, making it clearer. They had heard criticism when the bill was first introduced that young people wouldn't understand the graduation data, so they added a provision that a school's guidance counselor or principal would discuss it with the student athlete. And yet Bill wanted students themselves to have responsibility for signing off on the information. What should they sign?

The National Letter of Intent, provided by a college or university to a prospective student who is offered an athletic scholarship, is signed by the student to indicate his agreement, though

not binding, to attend that institution. Bill felt that the National
Letter of Intent could be the right vehicle for also signing off on
the graduation data. His new provision read that there would be
a space provided in the National Letter of Intent for that purpose.

In the House of Representatives, the bill had been assigned to
the Education and Labor Committee, whose chairman, Augustus
F. Hawkins of California, had referred it to his committee's smaller
Subcommittee on Postsecondary Education. On May 18, 1989, that
subcommittee began two days of hearings on the role of athletics
in college life and on H.R.1454, the Student Athlete Right-to-
Know Act. A variety of experts on sport and education spoke for
or against the bill, and when each finished he or she was questioned
by committee members seeking further information or opinion.
As the sponsor of the bill on the Senate side, Bill was invited to
address the committee, and he used this speaking opportunity to
sharply outline the legislation's need. "What is the problem?" he
asked rhetorically. "The problem is athletes who get scholarships
but who do not graduate. What is the dimension of the problem?
Nobody knows. The information is not available. Most impor-
tantly, it is not available to the families of the high school students
who are trying to make an informed decision about where to go
to college."

Bill also dealt with the objections he and his staff had heard
about the legislation. Yes, the NCAA should require this information themselves, he said, but they don't. "Now that this legislation is pending for a second time, the NCAA is talking about
releasing graduation rate data. Talk, but again no action has oc-
curred. The proposal for a plan at the 1990 meeting is, frankly,
too little too late.

"Now, other opponents of the legislation argue that it is too
hard for colleges to collect the data required by this bill. You know,
I find that to be a little lame. . . . The General Accounting Office
[GAO, an agency that does research for Congress] has completed

an investigation for this subcommittee on this issue and has found that the information could be compiled and reported.

"One final criticism that has been leveled at this bill is that it is too complicated for student athletes and their families to understand and that they do not really care about education anyway. Mr. Chairman, I frankly find that offensive hogwash."

In his prepared remarks, Ed Towns emphasized the scandalous treatment of student athletes by many colleges and universities. "Mr. Chairman," he said, "it's high time that we stopped treating our young athletes like gladiators who are thrown aside once their skills are no longer useful." Tom McMillen took a different approach. "In many ways this is a relatively innocuous consumer information bill designed to provide the students and parents with valuable information about the school they are considering. It is similar to the airline industry, which [by law] must report scheduling efficiency and the percentages of lost bags. Mr. Chairman, surely the education of our future generations is more important than a lost piece of luggage or a delayed flight." Months later, Ed Towns would recall that Bill's presentation and McMillen's lost-luggage argument would sway a lot of representatives to their side.

Nonetheless, the subcommittee decided to take a wait-and-see approach on the bill before recommending it to the full committee. Subcommittee members wanted to see what happened to the bill on the Senate side. They also wanted to see what the NCAA would do in 1990 about disclosing graduation rates (the NCAA wasn't scheduled to meet for another eight months). When Bill heard the news of the subcommittee's decision, he wasn't discouraged. After all, tax reform had taken six years to enact. He told staffers to keep him posted on when the bill would come before the Senate Labor and Human Resources Committee. Then he turned his attention to other legislative work.

6

THE BIRTH OF A LAW: PART II

ON TUESDAY, SEPTEMBER 12, 1989, the Senate Labor and Human Services Committee held its hearing on the student athlete bill. In support of it, Bill invited two well-known witnesses who represented the ideals the bill was striving for. One was Rollie Massimino, head basketball coach for Villanova University, who had graduated 100 percent, or all fifty-two, of his scholarship athletes in his sixteen-year career. The other was Oscar Robertson, the legendary basketball player who graduated from the University of Cincinnati, led the United States Olympic Basketball Team to a gold medal in 1960, and became a brilliant professional player inducted into the NBA Hall of Fame in 1980.

In all, twelve witnesses, including Dick Schultz, Tom McMillen, and Bill, would testify for or against the bill. By far the happiest among them was Rollie Massimino. At 3:40 that morning, his daughter had given birth to a healthy baby boy.

The start of Senate hearings on the Student Athlete Right-to-Know Act, September 12, 1989, in the Senate Labor and Human Resources Committee Room

The hearing, scheduled to begin in the Dirksen building's Labor and Human Resources Committee Room at 9 A.M., attracted a decent-sized crowd. Many of those present were Labor Committee or Senate staffers, but others were average citizens interested in seeing their government at work. With its cork floors, raised dais, and panelled walls, the committee room presented a typical Capitol Hill environment. Television cameras and their crews lined one side of the dais. Reporters for different newspapers from around the country occupied an entire back-corner table. In the space between the dais and the witness table no fewer than six press photographers snapped photos of the witnesses and their questioners. The Student Athlete Right-to-Know Act was definitely attracting media attention.

Shortly after nine, Senator Kennedy strode into the committee room, stood for photos with the chief witnesses, including Bill, then took his seat at the center of the dais. "We will come to order," he said.

After making introductory remarks about the history of the bill, Senator Kennedy turned the floor over to other committee members who might have comments. Senator Howard Metzenbaum, a third-term Democrat from Ohio, said that the issue of

Before the hearing started, Bill used his time to meet with witnesses Oscar Robertson and Rollie Massimino.

graduation rates had been raised with the NCAA five years ago, and they hadn't done anything about disclosing them. Of the bill he said, "I am sympathetic, supportive." Brock Adams, a first-term Democratic senator from Washington State, said, "We want to be certain that those who use superlative athletic talents in college . . . have the opportunity . . . to use their full talents after they have graduated. I commend you for the bill. . . . I am very much in support of it."

From the witness table, Bill spoke next. His statement was virtually a repeat of the one he had made before the House sub-committee in May, and he read only parts of it, requesting that the full statement be included in the printed record of the hearing.

Afterwards, the three senators asked Bill some familiar questions. Could the families of athletes obtain the graduation rates on their own? asked Senator Kennedy. No, said Bill, the information is not available. Would collecting the data create an undue burden on colleges and universities? No, said Bill, the GAO says it would take them about seventeen staff days. "That doesn't sound to me like a big burden," he said. And, said Senator Kennedy, if a college has a good graduation rate of student athletes, wouldn't they want to make that graduation rate known, to get more good athletes to enroll?

"I think that could be the biggest advertisement for . . . athletics in many schools," Bill replied.

To a question from Senator Adams about how graduation rates would be calculated, Bill explained that there are various ways to do it, but the legislation would require reporting on graduation rates over five-year periods. Once athletes on scholarship enter, "How many at the end of five years have a degree at University X? How many do not? . . . That is the requirement."

Oscar Robertson spoke next. "I graduated in four years," he said. "But during those days . . . you could not duck a subject. If you were in the school of business or marketing, or whatever, that is what you had to do. You had to take those courses." Today, he said, there are colleges where All-American football players take courses in basket-weaving. College coaches and presidents are accountable for the money that athletics produces, but they are "not accountable for the people who produce the money," namely the athletes. "I think this right-to-know act is really needed," said Robertson. Otherwise, there will be more and more former student athletes who cannot even read a menu, who will get out of school without degrees and with nothing to do.

For Rollie Massimino, the Senate hearing was an opportunity to explain Villanova's outstanding graduation record. "We ensure [every player's] success in the classroom by following what we have established as our Ten Commandments," he said. They include academic progress letters to the coaches on each athlete, weekly academic reports, mandatory study halls, full-time tutoring, and summer school.

Bill Bradley beamed as Coach Massimino delivered his testimony. He had asked the coach to testify because he knew he would deliver a powerful message, both to Senate and House members still undecided about the bill and to those colleges currently misusing athletes. The message was, if Villanova can have outstanding basketball teams and still graduate one hundred percent of its players, so can other institutions. And if an institution chooses not to follow Villanova's example, isn't it only proper that they should be forced to reveal their athletes' graduation rates so everyone can see their shameful performance?

The witnesses kept coming. Richard Lapchick, director of the Center for the Study of Sport in Society, Northeastern University, spoke supportively of the bill and stressed the importance of its requiring that graduation rates be reported by sport, gender, and race. "If I am a basketball coach," he said, "and I am recruiting a black male basketball player, he and his parents should have the right to know how other black male basketball recruits have done academically at my school. While it is good to have the overall data, it is in some ways irrelevant for him to know [how] a white male soccer player or a white woman field hockey star fared academically at my school."

Dick Schultz still argued that the NCAA could do the job of divulging graduation rates and pointed to recent rules the NCAA had adopted to improve an athlete's chances of graduating with a degree. One rule requires that high school athletes take college prep courses and meet minimum grade requirements in order to play sports in college. The other requires college athletes to declare a major and make progress toward a degree in order to continue their athletic eligibility. Schultz also argued that any graduation rate data should be adjusted to show the percentage of athletes who aren't thrown out of college, but who transfer to other colleges or drop out on their own. "If the athlete decides that he wants to drop out of school and pursue a professional contract, and he leaves

Bill begins his testimony.

Dick Schultz, executive director of the National Collegiate Athletic
Association, testifying before the Senate committee

in good standing, that should not be the responsibility of the institution," Schultz said.

Finally, he expressed concern about reporting graduation data by race and gender. Doing so, he said, might violate a law called the Buckley Amendment, which prohibits private information about a person being made public. For example, Schultz and others argued, in a given year if only one black male senior on a college's basketball team graduates, won't divulging the graduation rate for black male seniors that year violate that individual's right to privacy?

Bill was ready for Schultz's objections. During the question period he told the NCAA that if it wanted "to do a little special study on transfer [students]," then do it. If it wanted "to do a little special study on the kids that were given athletic scholarships and dropped out, do a little special study on that. But we want to have the best information."

Then he asked Schultz to suggest ways for the committee to deal with concerns about the Buckley Amendment. "What if you did it on a kind of rolling average of three or four years?" said Bill. "Would that not help?"

MR. SCHULTZ: Our researchers have suggested that a four-year rolling average might be much more accurate, and it would absolve the concern about the Buckley Amendment.

SENATOR BRADLEY: So that might be one way to handle your concerns?

MR. SCHULTZ: Right.

SENATOR BRADLEY: And you would recommend that, if the committee went ahead, we do that [use rolling rates], would you?

MR. SCHULTZ: In fact, I think that is something we even need to look at in our own data.

SENATOR BRADLEY: Yes. What if the person who signed a letter for a scholarship agreed to share his own information as part of the scholarship?

MR. SCHULTZ: That would be no problem.

SENATOR BRADLEY: So that is another way to handle [the privacy question]?

MR. SCHULTZ: That is correct.

SENATOR BRADLEY: Okay. So, the Buckley objection is not insurmountable if people of goodwill sit around the table.

MR. SCHULTZ: It is not an objection. It is just a question that needs to be resolved.

SENATOR BRADLEY: Right. I think it is a good question, and I appreciate your willingness to make the suggestions today.

With that exchange, the NCAA's objections crumbled. Bill had demonstrated that the student athlete bill could be made workable. Tom McMillen reinforced Bill's comments with his own eloquent testimony, and at the end of the hearing, Senator Metzenbaum said, "I think you will see some action here in the Senate. I hope we will see some action in the House." On the Senate side, the next big hurdle for the bill was markup, that is, its approval by the Labor and Human Resources Committee. Bill was optimistic that a majority of the committee's sixteen members would approve the bill. In fact, he and Ted Kennedy thought committee approval might be unanimous, which would strengthen the bill's chances when it reached the Senate floor.

IN THE SEVEN WEEKS between the hearing and markup, S.580 was given yet another overhaul. The rewrite, incorporating suggestions made during the hearing, was performed by Terry Hartle, chief education advisor for the Senate Labor and Human Resources Committee. A number of Terry's changes were significant. For example, in the earlier version of the bill, the National Letter of Intent, or NLI, was to have included a section with graduation rate data for a high school athlete to review and sign off on. But a witness at the hearing pointed out that the letter was only used by NCAA schools, not by the NAIA. "Is the NAIA to be excluded?" the witness asked. The answer, obviously, was no. So Terry, working with Ted Kennedy and Bill, threw out the old

Terry Hartle, education director for the Senate Labor and Human Resources Committee, was responsible for incorporating Ted Kennedy's and Bill's revision into the final draft of the Student Athlete bill. He did his rewrite on computer and then sent the revision to the Government Printing Office in Washington, D.C., for reprinting.

section and substituted new language that made no mention of the NLI. With that change, Bill gamely saw his requirement that a student sign off on the data disappear.

Also, responding to Dick Schultz's concerns, Kennedy and Bill had Terry draft a provision allowing institutions, if they wished, to provide information about voluntary dropouts and transfer students (Bill's "little special study" idea). And, since the hearings showed that the five-year graduation rate of some institutions was poor because many of their students were part-timers or transfers who needed more time to complete degree requirements, Bill and Kennedy had Terry lengthen the time period covered in the data from five to six years. The graduation rate would be reported as a rolling average, meaning it would be recalculated in six-year blocks every year. (For junior colleges, graduation rates would be reported as a three-year rolling average.)

Finally, the earlier version of the bill had required graduation rates to be reported separately for every sport. Since further research had revealed that the real problem sports were football and basketball, a new provision was written requiring four-year graduation rates for each of those two sports, and a separate graduation rate covering all other sports combined.

With all the word and provision changes, Terry recommended that the rewritten version of the bill be substituted wholesale for the draft version, and Bill and Kennedy agreed. So did the Labor and Human Resources Committee. On November 1, 1989, the committee voted fifteen to one to adopt the amended version of the bill, which meant the committee was recommending that it be considered for vote by the entire United States Senate. The bill had cleared a big hurdle. Immediately after the markup session, an exuberant Ted Kennedy strode to his committee office and phoned Bill with the happy news. "We did it!" he said, flashing the signature Kennedy grin.

Bill expressed his warm thanks. He knew that without the support of his colleague from Massachusetts, the bill could not have survived this far.

BY EARLY JANUARY 1990, supporters of S.580 turned their attention to Dallas, Texas, where the NCAA was holding its annual convention. Bill wanted Congress and the nation to know that, even if the NCAA adopted its own right-to-know legislation, he would pursue his bill for non-NCAA schools. The question was how to communicate that position.

After nearly twelve years in the Senate, Bill knew that the easiest way to get such a message into every major newspaper in the country was to attract reporters to a public event. Thus, on January 8, as the NCAA began its meeting, Bill staged a small-scale media blitz. He spoke to a group of young athletes at a high school in New Jersey, emphasizing the importance of academics over athletics, and explaining the desirability of his bill. The students got the message, but, just as important, so did the newspaper and television reporters assigned to cover Bill's appearance.

Bill then went to Rutgers University in central New Jersey to answer questions about the bill at a press conference. His New Jersey press secretary, Rona Parker, had had no trouble finding coaches and athletic directors from around the state to speak on behalf of Bill's legislation. Bill was joined at the press conference by eight supporters, including Princeton's men's basketball coach Pete Carril and U.S. women's Olympic basketball coach Theresa Grentz. Practically every remark Bill made at the press conference he had made many times before. But as he says, if you're trying to get legislation passed, "you must develop consistency and repetition. If you believe you're going to get something done the first time you speak it, you're going to be a frustrated and disappointed senator. You have to like what you're saying because you're going to have to say it over and over again. You *seek* repetition."

Bill got his desired result. His remarks at the high school and at Rutgers were carried on the wire services to major newspapers in all fifty states. When, the next day, the NCAA adopted its own right-to-know requirements modeled on the Bradley-Towns-McMillen legislation, Bill's response to the action became an important part of the story. "I am very pleased by the NCAA's action today in Dallas," he told a reporter for the *New York Times*. "[It] is fully consistent with the legislation that we have sponsored. While I am pleased at the action taken by the NCAA, I intend to pursue my legislation for non-NCAA schools, since there are hundreds of colleges in other athletic conferences not covered by the NCAA regulations."

The blitz served an added purpose. It reminded senators and congressmen that Bill's legislation was popular in the media. Politics is the art of persuasion, and Bill, as much as anything, was

January 8, 1990. As the NCAA met in Dallas, Bill went to New Jersey to gather media attention for his Student Athlete Right-to-Know Act. In one whirlwind morning, he spoke in support of it at a public high school, before television news cameras, and at a press conference at Rutgers. "As a senator," he says, "you seek repetition."

trying by his blitz to persuade his colleagues that voting for S.580 made good political as well as educational sense.

As Congress reconvened, though, the question was how to get the bill onto the Senate floor. Determining which pieces of legislation get voted on is one of the tasks of the Senate majority leader, who works with the Senate minority leader to draw up legislative calendars. All indications from the majority leader's office were that the legislative calendar was full. No one could find a way to put S.580 on the schedule.

Then, one day in late January, Terry Hartle from the Senate Labor Office phoned Ken Apfel, Bill Bradley's legislative aide responsible for tracking the bill. "Listen," said Terry, "the president's Excellence in Education Act is going on the floor next week. How would you feel about getting S.580 on the floor by tacking it to the Excellence Act as an amendment?"

"We'd like that a lot," said Ken Apfel. S.695, the Excellence in Education Act, was sponsored by the president "to promote excellence in education by recognizing and rewarding schools, teachers, and students for their outstanding achievements, enhancing parental choice, and encouraging the study of science, mathematics, and engineering." Though the Student Athlete Right-to-Know Act was an entirely different bill, Senate rules allowed the attachment of one bill as an amendment to another if members so agreed. Ken Apfel ran the idea past Bill, who also saw its possibilities, and Terry Hartle checked it with Ted Kennedy, who agreed. On February 6, on the Senate floor, Bill proposed his legislation as an amendment to the Excellence in Education Act. Up till then, several senators had placed "holds" on Bill's legislation, meaning that they had concerns about it and wished to delay its passage in the Senate. Says Ken Apfel: "Putting our bill up as an amendment to a bigger bill was a way of seeing if the senators who had holds on ours really meant it."

Fortunately, they didn't. With a little persuasion from Bill's office, the senators removed their holds, and the next day, the

Senate passed the Excellence in Education Act, which included Bill's amendment, by a vote of ninety-two to eight.

Now the stage was set for Bill's amendment to be passed as a separate measure. At Bill's request, and by agreement between the majority and minority leaders, a phone call went out on February 19 from the Democratic and Republican cloakroom secretaries to every Senate member, asking if they would agree to pass the student athlete bill by unanimous consent. Any senator who did not agree had until the end of the day's session to telephone his "no" vote to the cloakroom. Otherwise, if no one called, the bill was "cleared," meaning it was passed.

At the end of the session, Ken Apfel received a call from the Democratic cloakroom. Not one senator had called in a "no" vote. The Student Athlete Right-to-Know Act had been passed by unanimous consent. Its next stop was the House of Representatives, where, as Bill had learned from previous experience, *anything* could happen to a bill. Still, Bill felt that its going to the House in two forms improved its chances of adoption there.

WHAT HAPPENED WHEN THE bill reached the House was surprising, but, to Bill and Ted Kennedy, not at all unexpected. The publicity surrounding the Student Athlete Right-to-Know Act made it a magnet for other legislation floating in the House of Representatives. In March, the House Subcommittee on Postsecondary Education had held a hearing on something called the Crime Awareness and Campus Security Act. This was another consumer information bill for students and their families that would require colleges and universities to disclose facts about crime on campus, and would permit institutions to inform the victims of campus crime about disciplinary actions taken against the wrongdoer. To many on the subcommittee, lumping the student athlete bill with the campus security bill made sense, and that is what the subcommittee decided to do. But then came further action. The subcommittee—and later the full House Committee on Education and Labor—raised the question Ted Kennedy had raised two years earlier. They said, Why stop with student athletes? Why not require colleges to report graduation rate data for *all* students, so that *anyone* considering a college will know his chances of graduating from there?

Suddenly, an idea that once had seemed a long way off had arrived. With agreeable surprise, Bill and Ed Towns saw their smaller bill mushroom into something bigger:

1. A right-to-know bill for students
2. A right-to-know bill for student athletes
3. A right-to-know bill for those concerned about campus security and campus crime.

The Student Right-to-Know and Campus Security Act sailed through the committee, and then, on June 5, through the House of Representatives. The message to the Senate from the House: Not only have we passed your bill, we've passed something bigger. How about you? Will you pass it, too?

It was now the Senate's turn to act. Terry Hartle says, "In the spring, when the House Ed. Committee suggested a bigger bill, we said, 'Great!' We'd been hoping for one eventually—we just didn't expect such a quick uptake. Then, once the bigger bill was passed in the House in June, the Senate had three choices. It could vote on the House bill as received; it could go into conference with the House, using our smaller student athlete bill against their bigger, more comprehensive one; or we could pass our own Student Right-to-Know and Campus Security bill and bring it into conference with their bill.

"We felt we would be in a much stronger position going into conference if we adopted our own larger bill, and that's what we did. We took certain things out of the House bill that we disagreed with, and added things of our own. By then, too, the administration, meaning the president of the United States and his legislative

BILL BRADLEY

U.S. SENATE '90

As the Student Right-to-Know and Campus Security Act was being passed, Bill's reelection campaign was in full swing. Here, a campaign poster by artist LeRoy Neiman.

advisors, had contacted our office with their ideas for a bill, and we tried to incorporate those into what we produced."

Almost as quickly as in the House, the Senate Labor and Human Resources Committee, and then the Senate itself, passed its own version of the bigger bill. It was September 1990—two and a half years since Ed Towns and Bill Bradley had first met to talk about legislation for student athletes. Now there were two versions of the bill, and the House of Representatives had a choice. It could vote to accept the Senate version of the Student Right-to-Know and Campus Security Act, or it could request a conference to iron out differences between the two bills. (It could also refer the Senate's bill to the House Education Committee, or vote to amend the Senate version of the bill and send it back to the Senate, but those actions would waste time, which was running out for the 101st Congress.)

As expected, therefore, the House requested a conference, and the general sentiment was that differences between the two bills could be ironed out on the staff level. In mid-September, four Democratic and three Republican staff members were selected to represent congressional conferees from the House Education and Labor Committee, and five Democratic and four Republican staffers were selected to represent Senate conferees from the Senate Labor and Human Resources Committee. They met three times, starting on Friday, September 14, and they went through both versions of the bill section by section, line by line. Each side showed a willingness either to accept a section from the other side over their own (this is called "receding"), or to find a compromise agreeable to both sides. For example, the Senate bill required information on graduation rates to be made available starting October 1, 1993. The House's version required the same information to be made available starting July 1, 1992. The conferees compromised. They agreed in conference that graduation information would be made available beginning July 1, 1993.

There were numerous other compromises. The Senate bill called for graduation rates to be reported for football, basketball, and all other sports combined. The House version required, in addition, graduation data for baseball, cross-country/track, and ice hockey. The Senate conferees receded, accepting the House version, but added an amendment deleting ice hockey from the list.

In all, there were fifty-eight recedings or compromises reached, with one of the biggest having to do with the disclosure of a college's earnings from athletics. The House version required colleges to make such disclosures; the Senate bill didn't. The conferees discussed this one long and hard. They finally agreed to require the U.S. secretary of education, in conjunction with colleges and universities, to study the matter further and report his findings to the Senate and House by April 1, 1991.

"The conference bill was really a blending of the House and Senate bills," says Terry Hartle, the conferee representing Ted Kennedy for Senate Labor and Human Resources. "When all is said and done, we touched the student athlete title of the bill very, very little. When we were through, there was general agreement that we'd produced a good bill, one that even lobbyists for the education community were satisfied with."

So good was the bill, so agreeable was it to Democrats and Republicans, to college officials and athletic conference executives alike, that it was not even debated on the Senate floor. On October 22, 1990, the House adopted the conference report on the bill by voice vote. On October 24, the Student Right-to-Know and Campus Security Act cleared the Senate by unanimous consent.

"It's going to be made into law," said a pleased Marcia Aronoff, Bill's chief legislative advisor, and it was. Within a few days of its congressional passage, the final version of the bill was printed on thick parchment and delivered by messenger to the White House for the president's signature. Without ceremony, and with only a few of his advisors present in the Oval Office, President George Bush signed the bill into law on the morning of November 9, 1990.

For Bill Bradley, the passage of the Student Right-to-Know and Campus Security Act was a source of great personal satisfaction. He had sponsored a landmark bill and seen it enacted. He had given something back to academics and to amateur sport. Around his office, staffers experienced a lightheaded feeling from actually having gotten a law passed. It was a feeling not long savored, however. On Capitol Hill, Congress and the president were struggling to pass a compromise budget, while back in New Jersey, Bill was involved in the toughest Senate campaign of his political career. Issues other than the rights of student athletes were on the minds of Bill's constituents. What effect those issues would have on Bill's reelection remained to be seen.

7

A DAY

"Is the senator here yet?" a worried young woman asks Michael Jones, Bill Bradley's Senate press secretary.

"No," says Jones, smiling reassuringly. "But I expect him any moment."

"He knows we start at nine o'clock?"

"He knows."

The woman nods and disappears inside the front door of the Washington Court Hotel. Jones resumes his pacing on the sidewalk. He assumes that Bill has gotten stuck in traffic after dropping his daughter, Theresa Anne, off at school. It happens all the time. Four years earlier, Bill and his wife, Ernestine, observed that Bill's Senate work was impinging on his role as a father. "Bill realized that Theresa Anne was growing up and he was missing her childhood," she said. So they worked out a plan. Theresa Anne would live with Bill and go to school in Washington, where the family

74

Bill enters the Washington Court Hotel to speak on behalf of the United Nations Convention on the Rights of the Child. Behind Bill is his Senate press secretary, Michael Jones.

now owned a house near Embassy Row, and Ernestine, a professor of comparative literature at Montclair State College in New Jersey, would stay in Denville and commute to Washington by Amtrak for four-day family weekends. Bill thus became the primary caretaker, and though being apart is difficult for the Bradleys, it is a common hardship suffered by many senators and representatives and their families. Says one Capitol staffer, "You hear of people being elected to Congress and their families staying back in the home state, either because they can't afford to set up housekeeping in Washington or because the elected official's spouse won't leave a career at home. It's especially difficult for those representatives and senators whose home states are far from Washington and who can't commute easily. Some marriages don't survive. The schedule just takes its toll."

On this June morning, the only toll on Bill Bradley, as Michael Jones guessed, has been Washington's heavy traffic. On Capitol Hill, where the vehicle of choice among senators is often a Cadillac or Lincoln, Bill prefers the services of a 1980 Chevy Citation. It

zips into the hotel parking lot at 8:45 and Bill emerges from behind
the wheel, raising his eyebrows as if to say "I made it."

"How we doing?" he asks Jones.

"They're all set for us downstairs."

The two men enter the hotel and descend to its grand ballroom.
There, in the foyer, they are greeted by James Grant, executive
director of UNICEF (the United Nations Children's Fund) and
by Paula Jennings, media director for the World Summit for
Children Candlelight Vigils. In 1978, as its contribution to the
international Year of the Child, the government of Poland sub-
mitted to the U.N. a draft text of something called "The Convention on the Rights of the Child." In her book *In the Child's
Best Interest* author Kay Castelle defines a U.N. convention, or
covenant, as "a legal document setting out universally acceptable
standards, agreed among nations by consensus." The idea behind
Poland's document was to consolidate existing international law
on children's rights and to add standards to address more recent
needs of the world's children. Over a ten-year period, a forty-two–
nation panel from the U.N. Commission on Human Rights refined
the document, and in November 1989, it was adopted by the United
Nations General Assembly. For it to become international law,
however, it must be ratified by at least twenty countries.

This is where Bill Bradley comes in. Shortly after the General
Assembly's action, Bill's office received calls from UNICEF and
from Interaction, a group representing more than eighty private
voluntary organizations supporting the U.N. Convention on the
Rights of the Child. Based on Bill's long-standing sponsorship of
legislation helping children, they wondered if he would be interested in spearheading the effort in the United States Senate to
ratify the convention. *He certainly would*, came the reply. Could
he recommend a Republican senator who might be willing to serve
as cochair? Bill recommended Richard Lugar, a conservative Republican from Indiana and second-ranking member on the Senate
Foreign Relations Committee. In short order, Senator Lugar joined

Bill as a cochairman, and the two introduced legislation urging the United States' adoption of the convention. For any treaty or convention to be ratified, it must first be signed by the president, then passed by a two-thirds vote of the Senate. Bill Bradley is at a news conference in the Washington Court Hotel this morning to urge the signing and ratification of the convention.

In addition, today's news conference is meant to call attention to the candlelight vigils for children that will be held around the world in September, and to announce recommended goals for the leaders of more than seventy countries who will attend the U.N. World Summit for Children later that month in New York.

Bill is pleased to be part of such an undertaking. Having championed so many Senate bills concerning children's needs, including measures to reduce infant mortality and improve education, Bill feels this one is consistent with his other efforts.

There is a lively audience inside the ballroom. Many people present are representatives from the World Summit for Children Advisory Committee who want the convention to be ratified. Others are private citizens concerned about the plight of the world's children.

On the dais, Bill takes his seat next to Valerie Harper, the actress who is celebrity cochair with Jeff Bridges and Harry Belafonte for the upcoming candlelight vigils. They thank each other for their work on behalf of the summit and the convention, and then turn their attention to James Grant, who is beginning his opening remarks. The U.N. summit in September will be the largest in world history, he says. It is for children, and it has four goals. First, to stop children from dying needlessly at the rate of twenty-five thousand every day due to a lack of vaccines and vitamins. Second, to boost the Convention on the Rights of the Child, "this Magna Carta for our children, who are our future." Third, to spotlight those problems for which there aren't easy answers—"the millions of children that will die of AIDS in the coming decade. The debt crisis. The drug crisis." Finally, the summit is convening, says Grant, "to give a higher priority to children."

The next speaker, David Liederman, executive director of the Child Welfare League of America, says, "Here we are, the wealthiest country in the world, and our kids are in deep trouble. Child deaths are commonplace from abuse, neglect, murder in every major city in the country. Last year we had 2.4 million cases of abuse and neglect. Our poverty rates are off the board—we're the highest among eleven industrialized countries in the world. Fifty-percent school dropout rates in every major city in the United States. Can you believe that? The wealthiest country in the world and one out of every two kids in our major cities is dropping out of school?

"We need to shift priorities in this country—we need to shift priorities in every country in the world, but we particularly need to shift priorities in this country. . . . We need a big-time initiative for kids right here in the United States. . . ." It would be good, for starters, if the president called a meeting of the nation's leaders to decide what ought to be done for American children, he says. "It all starts right here in this town called Washington, D.C., and it's time to begin today."

Now it is Bill's turn. Knowing he would speak this morning, he drafted a brief speech last week before leaving for a weekend with his family in New Jersey. As he does for practically every speech he writes, he ran the text past a few of his closest aides, soliciting their comments and accepting or rejecting their criticisms. Now he removes the text from his jacket pocket, clears his throat, and begins.

"In the past month, we've seen some striking images that opened our eyes to how children are systematically abused throughout the world. Just think of the pictures that you've seen in the newspapers. In Romania, the newly elected government opened the doors on the horrible barracks in which [former prime minister] Nicolae Ceauşescu warehoused children, especially the disabled,

"Children are not put on this earth to be our laborers, our economic bounty, or our pawns in our wars. Children need to learn, to grow in peace and freedom."

retarded, and mentally ill children who did not serve his economic purposes. In Ethiopia, where just a few years ago our hearts went out to young victims of famine, now children are the bounty in a vile war of attrition. Cluster-bombing and napalming of villages have no other purpose or effect than the slaughter of children.

"Children are not put on this earth to be our laborers, our economic bounty, or our pawns in our wars. Children need to learn, to grow in peace and freedom. Romania and Ethiopia are not the only governments that deny children the chance to grow. Let's think of a few others. In India, a twelve-year-old boy works sixteen hours a day in a tearoom for twelve dollars a month. In Brazil, a younger child scrounges for food in a garbage dump. And in the United States, too many low-birthweight babies no larger than my hand are born prematurely because their mothers do not have access to prenatal care.

Bill fielding questions afterwards. To his right is Valerie Harper; to his left are David Liederman, executive director of the Child Welfare League of America, and James Grant.

"To allow children to grow and learn, we must together make them our priority. The rules must be clear to all nations. Children have a right to justice, to an identity, to an education, to health care, and to freedom from hunger. That's the purpose of the U.N. Convention on the Rights of the Child. With the force of international law it says clearly to all nations that *children must come first*.

"I hope that the children's summit and these candlelight vigils that will circle the globe will bring the world's nations together to ratify that treaty and bring us a new day when children will receive the respect and love and care that they deserve."

The applause that greets Bill's speech is loud and sustained. As he sits, Valerie Harper touches his arm and says, "That was great," and suddenly she is at the podium, speaking about the need for political will to end children's poverty and hunger.

During the question period, a reporter asks Bill specifically how people can keep today's efforts alive.

"In the United States," he says, "the most important effort that someone can make who wants to push along the efforts we've all supported and championed today is to get people to write the president of the United States to have him approve the U.N. Convention on the Rights of the Child and send it to the United States Senate where we can ratify [it]. . . .

"Once we have done that, of course, your job is just beginning if you're an American citizen. You then commit yourself to be scrutinized by the world as to how you kept your commitment to the children of this country. And that means a very sizable effort to make sure legislators and executive leaders know about the needs of health care and education that cry out to be addressed in this country today, in regards to children."

More applause.

IT IS NINE FORTY-FIVE. "Senator Bradley has other commitments and must leave us now . . . !" intones the emcee. A minute later, Bill and Michael are hoofing it out of the hotel. Along with another press staffer and a writer, they pile into Bill's car for a quick drive to Capitol Hill.

Bill's six-year term as senator ends this year, and he's running for reelection. He has just spent four days in New Jersey reviewing details for his upcoming campaign.

"What time did you get in last night?" Michael asks him.

"One-fifteen this morning," says Bill.

"What happened?"

"Our plane was grounded in that thunderstorm. We were on the runway at Newark from four-thirty in the afternoon until eleven-thirty at night. Seven hours. Tying the record set in 1982 at Washington's National Airport."

Everyone murmurs in sympathy. The writer asks, "Do you ever take Amtrak?"

Bill accelerates the car. "Not often enough."

He waves to the guard at the entrance to the Hart Senate Office Building's underground parking lot and adroitly parks in his personalized space. Just as his car and clothes say, "Don't judge me for what I have—judge me for what I do," so does his briefcase. In fact, it is not a briefcase at all, but a moderately worn maroon gym bag with the word "Samsonite" emblazoned on it in black letters. Into it he slings everything from senate documents to little cans of apple juice, which he brings to the office for snack drinks.

He lopes toward the garage exit. Inside the Hart Building's massive basement, with its fast-food restaurant and document-storage room, he nods to the Capitol policemen manning a metal detector and baggage X ray and takes an elevator marked "Senators Only" to his office on the seventh floor. Before him in the building's marble atrium, a huge black iron sculpture called *Mountain and Clouds*, by the late sculptor Alexander Calder, thrusts jaggedly toward the skylights, its mobile of iron cumulus clouds turning slowly on currents of machine-cooled air.

Bill likes contemporary art. His own waiting room and office contain examples of photo-realism and abstract expressionism, and one of his first purchases as a professional basketball player was a silkscreen print by artist Roy Lichtenstein. In addition, his waiting room contains a half basketball that serves as both a pop art planter for a scraggly rhododendron and a tangible reminder of Bill's earlier life. Passing the planter, Bill says hello to the two young receptionists who in the course of a long day will greet some one hundred visitors and answer some eight hundred phone calls. A similar volume of visits and calls occurs daily in every legislative office on Capitol Hill. Many of the callers and visitors are lobbyists—paid professionals hired by business, industry, and special interest groups—to plead their cases for or against different pieces of legislation to Congress members. Other callers are Bill's New Jersey constituents who seek his office's help in dealing with federal agencies. The lobbyists' calls are referred to appropriate legislative

Most senators, including Bill, park their cars in garages below the Hart, Dirksen, or Russell Senate office buildings. Instead of a briefcase, Bill uses a Samsonite gym bag.

assistants, who pass the lobbyists' concerns on to Bill for his consideration. The constituents' calls for help go to staffers who specialize in handling such casework. On a given day the staffers may help an elderly person track down a social security check, or a military veteran receive his medical benefits, or a bereaved family get clearance from the Immigration Department to receive the body of a relative who died overseas. In all, such casework can consume over a third of Bill's staff's time, and since 1979, his office has helped over one hundred twenty-five thousand constituents.

Chairman Bradley and Energy Committee counsel Tom Jensen

Passing through the waiting area, Bill moves to his own office
at the end of a warren of little cubicles. On his desk, his personal
secretary, Marina Gentilini, has left representative letters from the
more than three thousand pieces of mail that poured into his office
yesterday. Since Bill cannot possibly read every letter sent to him,
mail room staffers sort it by subject and show him samples so that
he can see, especially, how constituents' feelings are running on
different legislative issues. As is true of most senators, "it still
matters to Bill a lot that everyone gets some kind of written
response to a letter," says Marcia Aronoff, his administrative assistant. To that end, staffers draft response letters based on public
remarks Bill has made on different subjects, and Bill revises the

letters until he is satisfied that they accurately reflect his views. Once a letter is rewritten and approved by Bill, it is computerized and sent as a response to a constituent's written concerns. As impersonal as all this may seem, nonetheless, says Aronoff, "the response is all Bill's. The response he gives in writing to one person on a particular bill is not unlike the response he would give in person to someone else. In addition to people's feelings on issues, we get a huge volume of casework letters. Just opening and sorting the mail by categories takes an incredible amount of work."

For now, Bill has only enough time to glance at the stack of mail on his desk before reviewing the rest of the day's schedule with Marina and Marcia and then speed-walking to an energy subcommittee hearing in the nearby Dirksen building.

The hearing is for the Subcommittee on Water and Power, and Bill, as one of the ranking Democrats on the Energy Committee, is its chairman. He is also, today, the only senator of nine on the subcommittee to show up, but the absence of his colleagues neither surprises nor disappoints him. Bill knows firsthand that a senator's schedule is often so full of conflicting hearings and other meetings that he and his staff must choose where his presence is most needed. Besides, if a senator misses a hearing he can, like any U.S. citizen, obtain a written transcript of the hearing through the Government Printing Office or the Senate Document Room in the basement of the Hart building.

The hearing is on two pieces of legislation that have been referred to Bill's subcommittee. The first calls for a series of irrigation projects in South Dakota; the second, for a rural drinking water system there. Testifying on behalf of the bills are a number of South Dakotans, both prominent and little known, who have flown to Washington from their home state solely for this hearing. Bill listens sympathetically to what the witnesses have to say, especially two witnesses who paint a bleak picture of life in their region without water irrigation. Leo Holzbauer, chairman of a South Dakota water system, who favors the irrigation bill, says that the frequency of drought in his region is causing the migration of children from the family farms there. Stephen Cournoyer, Jr., chairman of the Yankton Sioux tribe, who also favors the irrigation project, says that *something* needs to happen to improve life on his reservation, where there is currently an 80 to 90 percent unemployment rate, the highest infant mortality rate, lowest life expectancy, and highest rate of diabetes in the country. "We are very much interested in seeing the [irrigation] project move forward, as it would be an opportunity to develop the only natural resources that we have," Cournoyer says. "We have become so used to disappointment and failure that it has often become difficult to look to the future. If we cannot get anything going out here, then what will the future hold? Social and economic problems double or triple what they are now?"

Bill praises the two men for the effectiveness of their testimony and calls them "kind of the best of what we have in the country." At the same time he points out that the governmental process of authorizing, reviewing, and finally constructing the irrigation project would likely take ten years or more. Bill's words have a sobering effect on everyone in the committee room. He hopes the Senate can be helpful in legislating what the South Dakotans need, but he cannot be optimistic about speedy solutions.

Noon. While Bill has been speaking on behalf of children's rights and chairing a hearing on water projects, the Senate has been in its day's session since nine-thirty this morning. Five glowing lights on the clock at the back of Bill's committee room now indicate that senators have seven and a half minutes to go to the Senate floor to vote on a matter there. Since it is impractical and unnecessary for senators to be in the Senate chamber during every minute the Senate is in session, a system of lights and buzzers exists to alert them when their presence is required. In addition, closed-circuit cameras, installed in the Senate gallery in 1986, now allow senators' offices to monitor the proceedings by television. In Bill Bradley's senate office, as in most others on Capitol Hill,

Stephen Cournoyer, Jr., chairman of the Yankton Sioux tribe, testifying in favor of an irrigation project that would improve life for his reservation.

legislative staffers usually find themselves keeping one eye on their immediate work, the other on their television screen in case something happens in the Senate that requires their boss's attention.

In this case, Bill's vote is required on an amendment to remove the Social Security trust fund from calculations of the national debt. Bill knew last week that the vote on the amendment would be today. He saw the notice in the legislative calendar circulated by the Senate majority and minority leaders. The advance warning served to give Bill and his colleagues time to study the amendment and decide which way to vote. Now, after phoning his office to confirm the vote is on, he takes an elevator to the Dirksen basement, where a Senate subway car whisks him and several other colleagues to the Capitol. There, he takes an elevator to the second floor, enters the Democratic cloakroom, and passes through a set of swinging doors into the Senate chamber itself.

There are about one hundred spectators in the gallery. Many nudge one another and whisper, "That's Bill Bradley!" when he appears on the Senate floor. The assistant legislative clerk, who knows all one hundred senators by sight, spots Bill immediately and, as his position requires, calls his name.

"Mr. Bradley . . . !"

With that acknowledgment, Bill casts his vote on the amendment. "Aye!"

"Mr. Bradley votes 'aye'!"

When the roll-call vote is tallied, the ayes (or "yeas," as they're called) outnumber the nays ninety-six to two, with two senators absent and not voting. The amendment passes. It is twelve-thirty. Bill and the fifty-four other Senate Democrats now troop to the Senate caucus room for their weekly private discussion on legislative strategy. There, the Senate majority leader solicits the views of his fellow Democrats on which pieces of upcoming legislation they favor and which they do not, on which they would like to support, but, for various reasons, cannot. At times, Bill has found himself alone in his views on certain legislative issues such as tax reform or, at one time, aid to the Nicaraguan *contras*. Disagreeing with others, particularly when they are members of your own political party, is never pleasant, but Bill accepts disagreement as part of his job as senator. He says, "My parents always taught me . . . the value of being independent, doing what's right, standing by my convictions, even when I'm under assault, even if I lose sometimes." Fortunately, there are no assaults at today's Democratic conference, and at one-thirty Bill is back in his office, in time for a fifteen-minute interview with a children's book author who is writing a book about him.

At two o'clock Bill is scheduled to go to a meeting of the Select Committee on Intelligence to be briefed by White House officials, Central Intelligence agents, and United States military leaders on sensitive activities abroad, but for one reason or another that meeting has been cancelled, freeing Bill to work on a speech he needs to deliver tomorrow morning on the Senate floor. The speech is on a constitutional amendment proposed by President Bush that

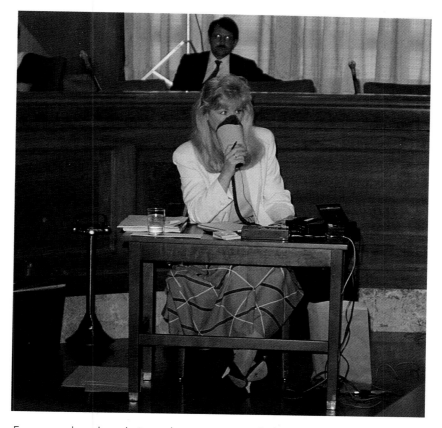

Every word spoken during a hearing is recorded, transcribed, and printed in the form of a report. Here, the recording technician uses two tape recorders—one that records voices directly, another to record her near-simultaneous repetition of what she hears.

would outlaw burning the American flag, and the issue has become an explosive one, both in the Senate and around the country. Many Republican leaders, including President Bush himself, are using the issue as a way of questioning the patriotism of their Democratic opposition. In effect they are saying that if a person opposes the idea of a constitutional amendment against flag burning, he must not be a real patriot because, after all, real patriots would naturally support such an amendment. In New Jersey, where Bill is running for Senate reelection, his campaign office is reporting that his

Subway cars connect the three Senate office buildings to the Capitol itself. Anyone admitted to the buildings can ride the cars for free, but senators always have first priority.

Near the end of a long day, Bill spots a colleague in the atrium of the Hart building.

Republican opponent has begun asking where Bill stands on the issue of flag burning. Is he for a constitutional amendment or against it? Does he have a position or doesn't he? When is he going to reveal it? The people of New Jersey have a right to know.

For many reasons, Bill opposes a constitutional amendment against flag burning, but he also opposes flag burning itself, and he resents any suggestion that he might be unpatriotic. He knows the time has come to speak out. He has written a rough draft of the speech, which, as usual, he has shown to his closest advisors. Now he shuts himself in his office for the next few hours to polish the speech so that it says exactly what he wants it to say, and also leaves no question about where he stands on the issue and why. At four-fifteen, he will meet with the chairman of the Port Authority of New York and New Jersey to discuss transportation issues facing the Northeast, but his main focus throughout the afternoon and evening will be on the speech. The day has not been an atypical one. If Bill feels he has the time, tonight he will attend a congressional reception sponsored by the Port Authority at a nearby Washington hotel. Otherwise, he will go home, have a light supper with Theresa Anne, phone his wife, work some more on the speech, read committee reports on upcoming pieces of legislation, make telephone calls to his legislative and campaign staffs, and call it a night at around twelve-thirty.

Bill has said that, compared to playing pro basketball, being a senator is much more a constant grind with many more constant pressures. Still, he considers his work "a remarkable opportunity to contribute to the life of our country." It is work that often leaves his face drawn with fatigue and his body hurting for exercise. To unwind on days when his schedule permits, he rides a stationary bike in the Senate gym for thirty minutes and does some calisthenics. Only rarely does he shoot baskets, and then it's only with his daughter or alone.

8

THE SOVIETS

In 1964, when Bill Bradley was captain of the U.S. Men's Olympic Basketball Team, he knew the U.S. would likely play the Soviet Union in the finals. To prepare for the contest, Bill went to a Russian professor at Princeton and asked for a few words of Russian that he might use on the court.

"What sort of words?" the professor asked.

Bill said, "How about 'Hey, big fella! Watch out!' "

The professor gave him the words.

Sure enough, the finals matched the Americans against the Russians, and Bill's opponent, Yuri Korneyev, at six feet five inches and two hundred forty pounds, outweighed Bill by forty-five pounds. About eight minutes into the game, Korneyev gave Bill a hard elbow in the chest and throat. Bill staggered backward, but then remembered the Russian words. Gathering himself, he shouted, "Balshak, astarozhna!" Korneyev fell back, stunned.

At a mosque in Tashkent, Uzbekistan. The cap and jacket were a gift to Bill from the local Moslem leader, called a mufti.

"A funny thing happened after that," Bill says. "Up until that moment the Soviets had been calling all their plays verbally. After that moment not only did they stop calling all their plays verbally, they stopped talking to each other!" The Americans went on to win the game and the gold medal, and Bill never forgot this lesson in international preparedness.

Since that day in Tokyo in 1964, Bill's interest in the Soviet Union has only deepened. He made his first Soviet visit while at Oxford, in 1966, and over the past twenty-five years has continued to make periodic visits there, both to learn more about Soviet society and to observe its politics and economy firsthand. As a senator he has traveled five times to the Soviet Union, starting in 1985, and each trip has been jammed with meetings and discussions interspersed with whirlwind visits by plane and car to the country's remotest reaches. Gina Despres, Bill's counsel and foreign affairs advisor, calls the trips "grueling," but says Bill is a "resilient" traveler. "I think his being able to withstand the rigors of the trips comes from his days as a basketball player, when he had to travel so much," she says.

Trips abroad to study other countries are a common feature of most senators' labors, and such travel is done at taxpayers' expense. Bill feels that, because of his work in the Senate on energy, intelligence, and international debt, it's his *duty* to visit the Soviet Union and learn all he can about it. In fact, he feels the Soviet Union is one of three countries that *every* American should know more about (the others are Japan and Mexico). He has met with everyone from Mikhail Gorbachev to the *mufti* of Central Asian Muslims. When a Soviet dignitary comes to Washington he's as likely to seek out Bill for a chat as he is any White House official.

For decades, under the dictatorships of Joseph Stalin, Nikita Khrushchev, and Leonid Brezhnev, the Soviet Union was a totalitarian state with one central party, the communists, that controlled all aspects of Soviet life. Soviet citizens were barred from spreading religious beliefs, printing or reading certain books, owning and operating their own businesses, criticizing the government, traveling freely, or generally exercising any of the freedoms that most Westerners take for granted. In the aftermath of World War II, the Soviet Union and the West, particularly the United States, found themselves opponents in what came to be known as the Cold War—an ongoing conflict just short of open warfare and characterized by ideological differences (communism versus democracy), espionage, sabotage, hostile propaganda, and the largest buildup of weapons, including nuclear weapons, that the world has ever seen. As late as 1982, President Ronald Reagan characterized the Soviet Union as an "evil empire" that could be contained only by increased U.S. military spending and developing an outer-space antinuclear system dubbed Star Wars. Every year, both the Soviet Union and the United States fell further into debt as each superpower tried to outdistance the other in military preparedness.

Then, in 1985, after years of economic stagnation and waste, a new Soviet leader, General Secretary Gorbachev, advanced three radically new ideas. The first was *perestroika*, a Russian word meaning "reform." Gorbachev proposed that the Soviet Union should seek to reform its centralized, government-owned and government-controlled economic system and encourage instead the development of privately owned and operated businesses and a more internationally oriented economy. In addition, Gorbachev encouraged *glasnost*, which means "openness," or permission to speak out and criticize—a sharp departure from Soviet law requiring blind obedience to the state. Along with *glasnost*, Gorbachev also championed democratization of the bloated, corrupt, and lazy central government so that all Soviet citizens, particularly younger ones, might have a voice. By encouraging *perestroika, glasnost*, and democratization, Gorbachev was in effect admitting that, after nearly seventy years of iron rule, the Soviet communist system had failed. One day in Washington, Bill told a group of young Democrats: "My read on what's happening in the Soviet Union is that Mikhail Gorbachev woke up one day in 1985 and looked out at a Soviet Union that was in a state of disintegration. It had a rising adult and infant mortality rate. It had one hundred and two cities with populations of over fifty thousand where air pollution was ten times the Soviet national standard. It had massive needs for capital for everything from health care systems to industrial production to transportation. It was a society where crim-

At an American exhibit, Tbilisi, Georgia

On a street in Alma-Ata, Kazakhstan, as Bill was about to enter a building, an old man bowed to him. Bill bowed back. The man bowed again. Bill bowed. Before long, each was laughing delightedly.

inality was rampant. Along with that, people were losing faith in the system and feeling there would never be a better life for themselves and their grandchildren.

"I think Gorbachev looked out at that world and thought, 'I'm going to have to take some big risks and make some changes.' And he embarked on his series of reforms. . . . I asked a Soviet friend of mine how we'll know when *perestroika* has worked, and he said, 'You'll know *perestroika* has worked when more people want to get into the Soviet Union than want to get out of the Soviet Union.' Maybe that's an appropriate measure of advances there."

Bill's travels to the Soviet Union since 1985 have convinced him that, though *perestroika* may be having a rough time of it, *glasnost* is not. In 1985, Bill could scarcely say hello to average Soviet citizens on the street without encountering suspicion and silence. "It was still the Brezhnev Soviet Union," says Gina Despres, "an extremely grim, extremely oppressive place." By 1988, however, Bill found the government and citizenry more forthcoming. In Moscow, he was allowed to meet with refuseniks—people who opposed the Soviet government and were previously jailed for their views. Throughout the Russian countryside, he saw churches and synagogues that had once been closed by decree now bursting with people able to practice their religions once more. In Tbilisi, he held an impromptu town meeting where Soviet citizens asked him everything from his views on U.S. elections to details about his life as a basketball player.

By traveling to nearly all of its fifteen republics, Bill has seen firsthand that the Soviet Union is not a monolithic society comprised of one nationality, but instead is a rich mosaic of 169 different nationalities and more than 100 different languages and dialects. Within each republic can be a variety of religions, including Eastern Orthodox Christianity, Protestantism, Roman Catholicism, Judaism, Islam, and Buddhism. With all these religious and ethnic differences, the potential for conflict since *glasnost* is enormous.

Indeed, in 1990, clashes between Azerbaijanis and Armenians in Azerbaijan, and clamorings to secede by the republics of Georgia, Estonia, Lithuania, Latvia, and Moldavia, demonstrated the power of nationality issues in driving the Soviet Union's march toward reform. "Bill's travels to the U.S.S.R. showed him early on that nationality issues are really going to be dominant there," says Gina Despres. "Bill now feels that, to succeed at economic reform, the Soviets have got to resolve nationality and ethnicity questions first. But they must do so humanely, in a way that respects people's legitimate desire for freedom and self-determination."*

Bill's trips have also convinced him that the United States should be cautious about investing money in the Soviet economy. As he has said, "I think that we should applaud *perestroika*, but we shouldn't pay for it." Instead he feels our interests are better served by seeing more money in the Soviet national budget go to its civilian programs and less to its military programs. Sure, Western banks can lend money to the Soviet Union if they want to, he says, but they shouldn't come crying to the U.S. Congress to bail them out if the loans aren't repaid. "We should be rational capitalists, not romantic capitalists," Bill says, so that the Soviet Union doesn't become "the international debt problem of the 1990s following on the Latin American debt problem of the 1980s."

Perhaps more than anything else, Bill's Soviet travels have shown him that the people of the Soviet Union are just that— people—who want to understand our system of life and government as much as we do theirs. One day, Bill and eight other senators played host in Bill's Washington office to Boris Yeltsin, chief rival for power in the Soviet Union to Mikhail Gorbachev. After a lengthy discussion in which Yeltsin stressed the need for

---

* Indeed, when Soviet troops cracked down on the budding democracy movement in the Baltics in January 1991, Bill cosponsored a Senate resolution condemning the action and calling upon President Bush to review all economic benefits by the U.S. to the Soviet Union.

Bill in his outer office, greeting Boris Yeltsin. Behind Yeltsin is his Russian translator.

American investment in his country, Bill gave his Russian guest a tour of his outer offices. When they came to the mail room, Yeltsin's eyes popped. It seems that mail rooms—and mail itself —are scarce in Soviet politicians' offices. The idea of receiving so much mail and being able to answer it with computer-printed letters bedazzled Boris Yeltsin. He grinned and grunted. He was already late for a luncheon. Staffers began wondering, How are we going to get him out of here? Finally, like one who has stumbled over the threshold of another's wealth, Yeltsin thanked Bill for his hospitality. With a sigh, and a last longing glance around the mail room, he departed.

POSTSCRIPT

What a difference a year makes. When this chapter on the Soviets was written in the late summer of 1990, Boris Yeltsin and Mikhail Gorbachev were feuding political rivals, perestroika *seemed increasingly threatened by a hard-line communist backlash, and Gorbachev himself appeared to be trapped in a limbo between dictatorship and national reform. In January 1991, with Gorbachev's crackdown on freedom movements in the Baltics, and the subsequent continuing deterioration of the Soviet economy, the stage appeared to be set for an ideological showdown in the central government itself.*

That showdown came on August 19, 1991, when eight Soviet officials, each of them former Gorbachev colleagues, seized control of the central government, having put Gorbachev under house arrest the day before at his dacha in Foros, near the Black Sea. For three days a stunned world watched as the coup unravelled, the conspirators either committed suicide or were arrested, and Boris Yeltsin emerged as a popular Russian hero with a standing perhaps greater than that of Gorbachev, who returned to Moscow a chastened and nearly irrelevant leader. As this book goes to press, Soviet communism appears to be truly dead, the Baltic states of Lithuania, Latvia, and Estonia have won their independence from the Soviet bloc, and the remaining former Soviet republics are grappling with the question of how best to construct a new government.

Given his knowledge of the Soviet Union, Bill Bradley watched these events with intense interest. In the August 28, 1991, edition of the Washington Post *he wrote: "Events last week in the Soviet Union changed more than the colors of a nation's flag. They redrew the strategic map of the world." To ensure that the revolutionary changes are irreversible, Bill argued that the time is ripe for the West to provide "expertise and interim support to facilitate economic reform. But," he added, "let's be clear that we're trying to help the republics, not the Soviet Union. . . . The Soviet Union, like communism, may soon be history.*

"Any republic that requests help," he continued, "should receive from the international community—not just the United States—an expanded program of technical assistance, training, and educational exchanges" to build market economies so that the republics can compete in the global marketplace. Before funds for loans are released, Bill argued that the republics, either individually or collectively, should meet four conditions:

First, the republics must define their constitutional and economic relationship among themselves.

Second, they must create programs toward stabilizing themselves economically.

Third, they must create the structure of a democratic free-enterprise system.

Fourth, they must be prepared to protect the poorest and most vulnerable members from upheavals in the marketplace.

As for American investment in a new Soviet Union, Bill continued to argue for caution. It should depend on a number of things, he wrote: the speedy withdrawal of Soviet troops from Germany and Poland, the return of the Northern Territories to Japan, reducing aid to communist Cuba, revising obsolete arms reduction treaties to reflect a new harmony with the West, and cutting the Soviet defense budget. If these things happen, Bill wrote, then U.S. defense spending itself could be cut, creating "more dollars for democracy."

Bill closed with a creative idea involving Mikhail Gorbachev. He should be appointed the next secretary general of the United Nations, Bill wrote, "a position for which he is uniquely qualified. Nobel Peace Prize winner; author of glasnost, perestroika, *and the new world order. . . . What better candidate is there to head an institution whose best days lie ahead?"*

9

STUDENTS AS LEADERS

BESIDES WRITING LEGISLATION and trying to get it made into law, besides helping his constituents with their government-related problems, besides making speeches, visiting foreign countries, and performing the myriad other duties and obligations of a United States senator, Bill Bradley also organizes what he calls "outreach programs" for people in New Jersey, particularly its youngsters, to, in his words, "broaden their understanding and experience." The annual Student Athlete Conference is one such program. Another is the Young Citizens' Award night, which, every year, recognizes four hundred different high school seniors throughout the state. In Bill's words, the students who receive the award "are . . . not the best athletes, not the best students—just good kids" who have given something back to their communities. A third group of programs are Bill's annual High School Leadership Seminars. They bring nearly six hundred high school juniors from all

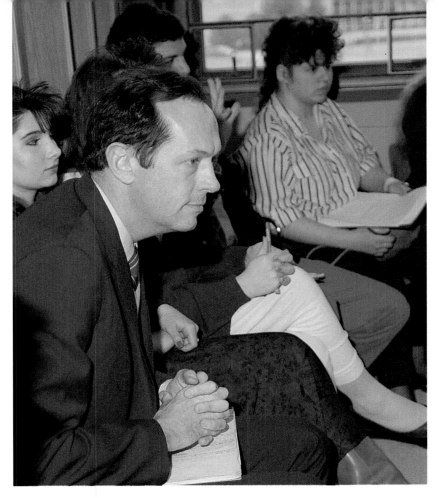

"You've got to think these things through, senators."

over New Jersey to three different college campuses in the state and ask the students to play the role of United States senator for a day and decide how to solve different domestic and international problems. Seminars are led by Bill's five legislative assistants, and Bill himself sits in on each session to listen, comment, and ask questions. "What Bill tries to do," says Marcia Aronoff, "is show students how complex a senator's decision-making process is, and how difficult it is for a senator to make a decision because of different competing interests. He feels very strongly that we have a special obligation to motivate and challenge young people. The seminars are one way to do it."

For the tenth annual seminar, which took place in February, the topics for discussion were "America's Role in the World,"

Ken Apfel: "Do you think the deficit is too big? Let's have a show of hands."

"Balancing the Budget," "Cleaning Up Toxic Wastes," and "Are Foreigners Buying Up America?"

Ken Apfel leads the discussions on budget balancing. For years, he explains to each group of about twenty students, the federal budget, which determines how much money our government will spend on defense, social programs, and federal services, has been running a deficit, meaning the government is spending more money than it raises through various taxes. "We have about a $150-billion-a-year deficit," Ken Apfel says. "To give you a sense of what a billion is: A billion seconds ago [in 1953], the Korean War had just ended. A billion minutes ago was roughly the Age of Christ. A billion hours ago, early man was just learning how to use stone tools. And the last billion dollars of the federal budget deficit has accumulated in the past two and a half days. The next billion will accumulate in the next two and a half days. Do you think the deficit is too big, and should we be doing something about it? Let's have a show of hands."

Every student in the room raises a hand. "This reminds me of the United States Senate," Ken says, "where the question of whether the deficit should be brought under control would receive a vote of one hundred to nothing. Yes, the deficit should be brought under control. The hard part is figuring out how, and what happens to the people affected by the programs where we cut money. How do you make choices? And what are the implications of those choices for all of us? This is what a senator has to wrestle with. All right. The first item on our list of possible cuts is Social Security, which provides monthly money for Americans at age sixty-five after they retire from their jobs, and which makes up about twenty percent of the budget. Do we cut it?"

A girl says no, because it wouldn't be fair to the retired people who have already paid into the system through taxes and through money withheld from their paychecks when they were working.

A boy says, "If we raise the age when a person could start receiving benefits from sixty-five, where it is now, to sixty-six or sixty-seven, I bet we could save a lot of money."

"Why doesn't the government only pay Social Security to those who need the money?" a girl asks. And a second boy says, "Heck, why not do away with government-sponsored Social Security altogether and let private insurance companies handle the program instead?"

Ken Apfel says, "There are three plans on the table: one, to raise the retirement age; two, to provide Social Security on a needs basis; and three, to scrap the plan altogether. Senators, it's time to vote."

While the budget-cutting process is under way, Bill has joined the seminar of his energy specialist, Gene Peters, on cleaning up toxic wastes. So far, the students have discussed what cleaning up toxic waste means and the various ways available for doing it.

They agree it can be burned, buried, dumped at sea, or shot into space, but it should be cleaned up and the production of new toxic waste should be reduced, perhaps by enacting laws that penalize the biggest producers.

Bill, who has been listening closely, now looks each student in the eye and says, "I want you to decide what you're going to do with this stuff. If you decide you're going to go the more expensive route and pick it up out of the landfills and so forth where it currently lies, I want you to tell me where you're going to put it. And then I want you to tell me who's going to pay for it."

The students fidget, realizing, perhaps for the first time, the enormity of their assignment. With a twinkle in his eye, Bill says, "You've got thirty minutes. You ought to be able to do that."

Meanwhile, in Marcia Aronoff's seminar, "Are Foreigners Buying Up America?", students are expressing their discomfort with the idea of countries such as Japan investing their money in the United States.

"Does it make any difference if the investment comes from abroad?" Marcia asks the group just as Bill enters the seminar room.

"I'm not sure," a student says. "Maybe the senator can answer my question."

"You're the senator," Bill says. "I'll answer questions later. Do you want foreigners to invest their money in the United States? Keep in mind, one of the things foreign investors buy from us is government debt. Our government runs a deficit, and then it floats a bond issue, meaning it sells government bonds, and foreign investors buy them, and we take their money and, for example, send it to you for student loans. Or to the Environmental Protection Agency to clean up the environment. That's how we finance our deficit. So if you say you don't want any foreigners to send their money here, then our government has to increase the interest it pays on those bonds to attract American investors. And I assume you don't want *that* increase to occur. So, is it maybe that you

"I want you to tell me where you're going to put it, and who's going to pay for it."

don't want foreign investors to buy American real estate, like Rockefeller Center? How many here care that a foreign investor has bought Rockefeller Center?"

A dozen hands shoot up.

"Why do you care?" Bill asks a girl.

"It's just the fact that we don't own it," she replies.

"Does it hurt us as a nation?" Bill asks.

"It hurts our pride, maybe," a boy says.

"Let's assume the worst," Bill says. "Let's say we fell out with the Japanese who have bought Rockefeller Center. What are they going to do with it?"

"Wipe it out!" a student shouts.

"Sell it!" yells another.

"Wipe it out, sell it," Bill says. "They might sell it, but to whom? Maybe to an American. Maybe to an American who

Marcia Aronoff: "Are foreigners buying up America?"

wouldn't pay as much. Maybe the Japanese paid too much to buy it in the first place. Why blame the Japanese? Why not blame Mr. Rockefeller, who sold it?"

"The Japanese wanted it for a reason," a student says.

"Riiiiiiight!" Bill nods. "What was it? Maybe they wanted to make *money*. . . . So you have foreigners investing in U.S. government bonds, and investing in properties like Rockefeller Center. And if you don't want them to invest in one, you don't want them to invest in anything?"

A girl says, "I don't think they should be allowed to own anything." A number of students nod in agreement.

"Okay," says Bill, "that's a point of view: foreigners should not be allowed to own anything in the United States. But, now, wait a minute: do we own anything abroad?"

The answer to the question is obviously yes. The students look sideways at each other.

"What if a foreign government told us that we had to pull our investments out?" Bill asks.

The students realize they have been caught in an inconsistency.

"You've got to think these things through, senators." Bill eyes the group. Then, as quickly as he entered the room, he rises and leaves.

He ducks into Gina Despres's seminar on America's role in the world and asks the students there what they feel about the relative merits of America's economic, military, and moral powers. "Which should assume the greatest importance in our dealings with the rest of the world?" he asks. "Is everything to be seen in economic terms? Military terms? And if you go down the moral route, don't forget, you have to avoid hypocrisy. Otherwise, you're the classic 'Do-as-I-say, not-as-I-do.' Which should be America's emphasis in foreign affairs?"

As the hour draws to a close, students in Ken Apfel's budget-balancing seminar have arrived at a consensus. They are prepared to make big cuts in spending on nuclear weapons, small cuts in spending on conventional weapons, and moderate cuts in domestic programs such as highways, agriculture, and outer space. They want to increase spending on student loans and education, and increase federal taxes on such "sin" items as cigarettes and alcohol. As for Social Security, the students decide to leave it alone.

Now Ken Apfel asks, "What would have happened if Senator Bradley had run this exercise with senior citizens?"

A student answers, "They would have cut spending for education because it doesn't apply to them and left money for Social Security and Medicare because they do."

Ken Apfel nods in agreement. "Here's something to think about," he says. "If you're a United States senator, you represent everybody living in your state. You have to try to balance out the priorities between senior citizens, who want their benefits; your parents, who feel taxes are too high; and you students, who want federal aid to education. And you have to be able to balance those

Bill and students continuing their discussion of domestic and international problems

three things with a need for national defense. *The job of a United States senator is trying to balance competing priorities in making decisions.* As you've seen, the choices aren't painless. And one of the reasons the debt is so high is because the choices are painful. I hope all of you keep an eye on your senators and your other elected officials—watch what they do, see if they stand for your values, see if they stand for the values of the state they're from, or the values of our country, or maybe the values of the world community. You did an honest job here today. Thank you for coming."

"I never realized how tough a senator's job is until today," a boy tells Bill when the discussion sessions end. "I want you to know I think of you as my role model. I play sports, I really work hard at my studies, and I'd like to go on to college and someday do the kind of thing that you're doing: helping people."

"That's nice to hear," Bill says honestly, and he can remember the impact that a student leadership seminar had on *him* as a high school student. "It's good to help others. But don't forget to do something for *yourself*."

"I won't," the boy says. "Thanks a lot."

A girl standing nearby, watching the Senator head to the dining room, says, "He is *so neat!* I wish I could be like him."

"Maybe you can," a reporter says.

"Naah," says a boy with mock contempt. "She doesn't have the jump shot!"

10

QUESTIONS AND ANSWERS

TOWARD THE END OF every student leadership seminar, Bill always schedules at least a half hour to answer students' questions. When the moment comes for him to launch into that phase of the program at this day's conference at Rutgers, he becomes playful and humorous. Grabbing the microphone off the podium, he says, "Now we're going into the town meeting portion of this program, where I come out from behind the podium"—he comes out from behind the podium—"where I throw the microphone cord across the room"—he flips the microphone cord across the stage like a pop singer—"where I jump down off the stage like Phil Donahue"—he jumps down off the stage like Phil Donahue—"and say"—thrusting the microphone under the nose of a surprised teenage girl seated at one of the luncheon tables—"WHAT'S *YOUR* NAME?"

Bill fields questions from high school students at one of his student leadership seminars.

The girl erupts in embarrassed giggles. The rest of the students roar. Bill shakes his head to show he's only kidding and says, "We're going to do a little question and answer session right now. You ask me any questions you want—you're my constituents— and I'll answer your questions. Then, at about one-forty I want you to answer an essay question: 'The Senator's comments were important because . . .' You'll have half an hour to do the essay; it'll count toward your high school graduation." The students laugh nervously. "No, no, no, no, no." Bill is only joking. "Don't worry, don't worry. Let's do some questions and answers."

A boy in a blue suit stands and asks, "Do you want to be president of the United States?" The students laugh and applaud. The boy has asked what Bill has come to call The Question. Since

1984, scarcely a week has gone by when someone—a reporter, a constituent, a passerby—hasn't asked Bill if he might one day run for the presidency. As early as 1963, Leonard Shecter, a columnist for the *New York Post*, wrote: "In twenty-five years or so our presidents are going to have to be better than ever. It's nice to know that Bill Bradley will be available." In his book about Bill as a student basketball player at Princeton, John McPhee quoted Bill's high school principal, Edward Rapp, as saying, "With the help of his friends, Bill could very well be President of the United States. And without the help of his friends he might make it anyway." Bill is flattered by suggestions that he run for the presidency, taking it as a recognition of his work in the Senate, but he gracefully declines to commit to such an idea, saying that, for now, he just wants to be the best senator he can be.

"You know," he tells the boy in the blue suit, "if I was a betting man, I'd have bet someone would ask that question." He pauses, looking into the students' expectant faces. "I like being your senator. I want to continue being your senator. People asked me in 1984 and 1988 if I was going to run; I said no. They asked why; I said I liked being a United States senator. They said, 'Why?' I said, 'Because it's not the right time for me.' They said, 'What do you mean?' I said, 'Well, I think the job deserves somebody's best—it is the most important job in the world.' They said, 'What do you mean by that?' I said, 'Well, I think somebody who's going to run for that office ought to have primary experience with as much of the country as possible. And that means understanding what it is to be a wheat farmer in North Dakota, because you've felt it a little bit; a coal miner, because you've experienced it a little bit; a stock trader in Chicago; a factory worker in Linden —so that you understand people because you've been there; you don't just read it out of books. You know because you've felt it and you've talked to people and you understand.' So I think you need primary experience of as much of the country as possible.

"Next, the president is commander in chief, head of national security. [To be president] you have to have knowledge that's tested against events over time. You can't be a great president simply if you have advertising slogans attached to briefing books. That [kind of knowledge] takes time.

"As president, if you're going to govern, you've got to have a big team, in and out of government, so that you can accomplish your purposes and they can hold you honest. [Fielding such a team]—that takes time.

"And then there's communication. I came from a nonverbal profession, let's face it."

The audience giggles.

"For ten years I didn't have to utter a word. I made a good living. All I had to do was run up and down the court—I didn't have to say anything. And now I'm in a profession where the only thing that's important is what I say. So I've had to learn.

"But the main thing is, I love being a United States senator. I don't think there's a better job in the world."

Another boy raises his hand. "You're running for reelection this year. If you're not reelected to the Senate, what would you do, go back to basketball?"

"Ahhhhhh!!!" Bill's eyes widen and his index finger shoots up. The students all laugh. "This man has asked the sixty-four-thousand-dollar question! I want the press to report today that I would be prepared to return in a minute if I am paid the average salary paid in professional basketball. When I came into pro ball, the average salary was nine thousand, five hundred dollars. The average salary today: a little over six hundred thousand dollars. So I'd be prepared to go back—just a spot appearance, you know—maybe a minute?" He smiles. "No. That period in my life is over. I wrote a book about that experience called *Life on the Run*. It's available in all your libraries."

The audience laughs.

"It's out of print. I kind of put that period in my life in perspective through that book. And if I wasn't in politics, I'd probably write. I'd probably continue to work with young people. I'd probably—oh, I don't know, a number of things. You don't want to peek at all your cards. I've got a few."

A girl asks, "What's the hardest part of getting started in politics?"

"Getting more than a hundred fifty people in a room," Bill answers. Then, turning more serious: "The most difficult thing [when I was] starting out in politics was understanding the breadth of issues that, if you're a serious politician, you have to master. For the first couple of years I was in the Senate, I didn't say too much. I was basically mastering the Senate procedure, the substance of my committees, and I was bargaining with my colleagues whom I had to get to do what I wanted them to do for New Jersey, if I was going to be successful. So [for me there was] that intense period the first year or two where I was moving from what is a very physical profession [basketball] to one that is very much a mental one [the Senate]."

"What do you like most about your job as senator?" a boy asks.

"I like most the fact that I can be a part—maybe somewhat superficially, but a part—of so many people's lives. I like being out with the people, listening to what they have to say. I like having the flesh and blood of my legislative work revealed to me in person. For example, I have been a big advocate in the Senate of the WIC program—that's the Women, Infants, Children feeding program. Well, there are a number of senators who are big advocates of the WIC program. I want to know how it works, though. So, at eight forty-five this morning I was in Elizabeth, New Jersey, and I visited a WIC program. And I went through the whole process, and I talked to a lot of people affiliated with it. And I now have an understanding about WIC that is deeper than if I was simply given a memo about it. I had that personal

In New Jersey Bill drives an Oldsmobile, which serves as his mobile office. Bill sits in the front seat and uses an old lapboard for reading, writing, and Senate paperwork. If there is food in the car it is probably a can of unsalted cashews. Says Hugh Drummond, Bill's driver: "Bill'll eat the whole can if you don't stop him."

experience, and that's what I like most: personal experience with the people I represent."

A girl raises her hand and says, "You're a member of the Democratic party, and yet your father was a Republican. Why did you choose the Democratic party?"

"I think for a couple reasons," Bill says. "First, through the study of American history, I came to believe that the Democratic party has been most responsive to the working people in this country who want a chance, and most helpful in assuring them that chance. Second, the civil rights period was very important to me. I was in the Senate chamber the night the Civil Rights Act of 1964 was passed. That was the first moment it dawned on me that maybe someday I might like to be in the Senate. And I think seeing [conservative Republican] Barry Goldwater cast his negative vote on that day labelled the Republican party to me in a way that I will never forget." He points to a boy at a back table. "Yes?"

"Do you have any regrets," the boy asks, "about starting your political career after your basketball career, and, if you had it to do over, would you have started your political career earlier?"

"Well," says Bill, "I almost ran for Congress in 1974, here in New Jersey, in a district up along the Delaware River. But I chose not to because I was in the middle of writing the book I mentioned earlier, I was earning a good living, I had just been married, I liked playing basketball still—my knees were not totally gone. And so I continued to play.

"As it turned out, everything was fine. In 1974, when I decided not to enter politics, people said, 'You're crazy! You'll never have another chance!' But, it turned out, I did have another chance, and with luck, and hard work, and help from friends, I managed to win election to the Senate in 1978. So I would not have entered politics earlier."

"Do you find it difficult to be dedicated to your Senate job and still have a family?" a girl asks.

"Yes," Bill says, "but my family comes first. I consider my children my primary responsibility because it's who your children are that is ultimately what you leave behind. And the family is also where I get recharged. In addition to interacting with people, having the private time to interact with the family is what, for me, recharges. But it is tough. My wife is a commuter. She teaches at Montclair State College, and she commutes back and forth to Washington. I commute back and forth to Washington and New Jersey. And it's a constant negotiation. But the idea is, the family comes first. And if you make sure that's the case, I think you, then, are a better senator."

"What advice do you have for a young person who may be interested in politics, who may even want to be a senator someday? What should he or she do?"

"This is a question I get in a lot of high schools and a lot of colleges," Bill says thoughtfully. "The most important thing you can do is learn how to write an English sentence clearly, and then learn how to put sentences together in paragraphs, and generally learn how to express yourself in writing and verbally. The second thing: learn something about American history and American literature, and know something about the world *before* you get into the nitty-gritty of politics. I'd say you have the next eight years in which you might not be directly involved in politics, but you can be building your own personal strengths so that if you ever *do* get into politics, you'll have something to say.

"Now, that doesn't mean you shouldn't get involved in a campaign sometime, just to get the feel of a race. But your quality time should be spent growing intellectually, learning how to write, how to communicate, understanding how things work, knowing yourself, so that you can bring more to the table should you ever decide to enter politics."

Bill now closes with a remark he often makes at town meetings with his adult constituents. He says, "I remember, twice in my life I stood courtside right before the final game of the world championship in basketball. The national anthem was playing, and I had chills going up and down my spine. And I thought to myself at that time, There is no place else in the world that I would rather be, and nothing else that I'd rather be doing. And that's exactly how I feel about being your U.S. senator."

11

BEACHWALK

AT PRINCETON, WHERE HE majored in history, Bill wrote his senior honors thesis on the 1940 Senate campaign of fellow Missourian Harry Truman. Later, Bill read more about Truman and learned that, when he became our thirty-third president, Truman liked to take daily walks outside the White House grounds to meet average citizens and hear their concerns.

Bill admires Truman. Upon his own election to the Senate in 1978, Bill promised to be as accessible as possible to his constituents. At first, whenever he could, he held town meetings throughout New Jersey. These were well received, but Bill recognized their limitation—namely, that people who wanted to see him had to go out of their way to do so. Then in 1982 he hit upon the Trumanlike idea of what he called the "walking town meeting." "It was simple," Bill says. "Instead of asking constituents to come to me, I'd go to where constituents are." In short order he began showing

Each August, Bill walks the beaches of New Jersey to meet constituents and hear their concerns firsthand.

up at places like New Jersey's Giants Stadium and New York City's Port Authority Bus Terminal, where New Jerseyans often pass at the rate of a hundred or more a minute. Like many politicians he went to county fairs, shopping malls, and city street corners. And, because its coastline is one of New Jersey's most valuable assets, Bill began setting aside time each August, when Congress is on vacation, to visit every beach in his home state. Traditionally he would start near Cape May in the south, and, over a period of several weekends, wend his way to Sandy Hook, one hundred thirty miles northward. In 1989, he decided to do the entire beachwalk in one five-day block, and his New Jersey staff rented a van so that reporters could travel with him on the first day's leg—Cape May to Atlantic City. During that day a children's book author kept a running diary of the experience. What follows are a few excerpts.

Robert Schoelkopf, director of the Marine Mammal Stranding Center in Brigantine, New Jersey, and Bill examine one of the center's patients, a Kemp's Ridley turtle rescued from the intake pipe at a nearby nuclear power plant.

AUGUST 15, 9:45 A.M. We're here at the Marine Mammal Stranding Center in Brigantine, New Jersey, waiting for Senator Bill Bradley to arrive and begin his day of beachwalking. He could've picked a better day for it—the sky is overcast and the air is brothy and heated. I suppose, though, even a senator can't control the weather. There are about a dozen reporters and three New Jersey–based TV crews here; apparently, media coverage of past beachwalks has been spotty, so Bradley's people have alerted all the newspapers and broadcast media in the state about this walk and rented a van for some of us to travel in. I ask a Bradley staffer why we're starting out from here and she tells me that Bill has been a personal supporter of the Marine Mammal Stranding Center, which was founded as a private nonprofit organization in 1976, and he applauds the center's work in rescuing seals, dolphins, and other marine animals washed up on Jersey shores. In addition, Bill has sponsored various pieces of legislation to ban the ocean dumping of medical waste and sewage sludge, she says. So, starting his beachwalk here is a way to call attention to that legislation and to the effects that pollution and other forms of human encroachment are having on our marine life.

Just then, Bill's maroon Oldsmobile rolls into the center's parking lot, and a serious-looking Bill Bradley emerges from the passenger side fresh from a two-hour drive from his home in Denville. He is wearing a red Ralph Lauren polo shirt, shorts, and Stan Smith tennis shoes without socks. He is greeted by Robert Schoelkopf, the Marine Mammal Stranding Center's director, who shows Bill and the rest of us one of the center's patients, a Kemp's Ridley turtle rescued from the intake pipe at a nearby nuclear power plant. A reporter asks Bill why he's here this year when it's not an election year, and he answers, "I've been doing this every year since 1982; it's just that you [the media] haven't noticed. I view this as a way of my showing concern for the shore, the quality of the water, and the beaches." He goes on to mention his medical waste tracking and anti–ocean-dumping legislation. As he talks, camera shutters clack and flashes wink in his face. Bill pays them no attention. As Schoelkopf would say later: "Bill's very honest and caring about what we're doing and what's going on with our oceans and beaches—even without cameras present."

10:20 A.M. THE VAN Inside the van, as it rolls south toward Cape May, Bill sits in the front passenger seat, silently sipping an apple juice and looking left and right at the coastal scenery. At Princeton, he was known to sports reporters as a "good interview"—someone who would willingly answer questions for hours. After a while, however, he grew weary of the repeated incursions on his time and into his private life, and, by the time he was a New York Knick, he came to be known as a "bad interview"—someone whose answers to questions were terse and perfunctory. Today, as a senator, he is neither a "good" nor "bad" interview, his response to questions perhaps best described as "businesslike." Still, at least one reporter has found that the quality of Bill's answers usually reflects the quality of the questions he is asked, as well as the reporter's degree of preparation.

Now a reporter in the van breaks the silence by asking Bill how he feels about next year's Senate election. Bill rubs his hand over his face and answers, "I take reelection seriously. I work very hard at my job and will continue to work hard." Another reporter shows him a newspaper story about ocean-borne counterfeit bills. Its headline reads "Funny Money Washes Up On Beaches." Bill skims it and, smiling, says, "What a difference a year makes," a reference to the previous summer, when used hypodermic syringes, blood bags, and other medical waste were washing up on shores from Cape May to Cape Cod. A third reporter asks Bill what he learns from talking to people on beachwalks, and he answers that he always gets a sense of people's intensity of feeling on different issues. For example, he says, early last summer he sensed right away people's intensity of feeling about the medical waste problem. "People, myself included, felt violated in a fundamental way by the medical waste that washed up on the shore. By the end of the summer, we passed the Medical Waste Tracking Bill and a bill to ban ocean dumping of waste sludge. That's an example where the intensity was there, and the response was there. I also like doing beachwalks because people stop and tell you stories. I find myself encountering more and more people approaching middle age who say to me, 'I remember you spoke at my high school.'"

Does he read the letters sent to his office? someone asks.

"Yeah, I do. Not every one, but as many as I can. Especially those where people tell stories. I don't read the postcards, though."

10:45 A.M. CAPE MAY   In an outdoor shopping plaza, two female Bradley staffers who have arrived in a separate car unfurl a large banner that in red letters reads "Come Meet Senator Bill Bradley." They start walking through the crowd of

Throughout the day Bill answered questions from the media. Over the years he has evolved from a "good" to a "bad" to a "businesslike" interview.

Bill's presence on the beach attracted a small army of reporters and photographers.

summer shoppers, and Bill follows about thirty yards behind. Suddenly all eyes seem to be turned toward the tall man in the shorts and polo shirt. People come eagerly up to Bill to shake his hand and say hello.

"How's it goin', Senator? Nice to see you!"

"Hello, Bill. I voted for you in 'eighty-four."

"Hey, Bill Bradley! The famous New York Knick."

Though a senator is not a magician, people still asked Bill to do something about the weather.

At every stop, Bill asked the lifeguards on duty about beach and water conditions.

"The beaches look good this year, Bill!"

"Hey, when you gonna run for president?"

Bill wades through the crowd, shaking hands and listening to people's comments. A baker from a nearby bakery offers a loaf of French bread, which Bill tries to pay for, but then, finding his pockets empty, politely declines.

"You goin' swimmin' today, Senator?"

"I might."

"Good luck to you, Bill!"

"Do somethin' about the weather, will ya!"

Bill raises his arms toward the sky as if to placate some angry weather god. Before long he has turned down a side street and soon is on the beach, shaking hands with people who seem content to be sunbathing in the dense fog.

"Where you from?" he asks a couple sitting in beach chairs.

"Montreal!" they sing in unison.

Bill makes a face. "How 'bout you?" he asks another couple.

"Toronto."

"Toronto!"

The fact that Canadians cannot vote in U.S. elections is not lost on anyone in the entourage. Reporters and photographers begin laughing. Bill rolls his eyes, smiling, and shakes his head. He churns up the beach, shaking hands with other beachgoers, at a speed that has reporters nearly jogging. At a lifeguard station he asks the two guards on duty, "How's the water?"

"A lot better than last year," they say.

"We've seen a few needles wash up on shore, Senator, but nothing like last summer."

Later, Bill explains to reporters that the Medical Waste Tracking Bill accounts for a half million pounds of medical waste that New York hospitals throw away every week. But, as he said to the lifeguards, "it can't stop diabetics and drug addicts from dropping needles in storm drains."

I I : 3 0 A . M . T H E V A N   A reporter notes that
many people at the last two stops asked Bill when he's going to
run for president. Is it like this everywhere he goes?

Bill fidgets, clearly uncomfortable with the question. "Not
really." He looks out the window. "It's just there."

Does he feel any pressure from the constant suggestions that
he run?

Bill turns back from the window, aware that the question is
not about to go away. "No. It's flattering." He pauses. "I take it
as a recognition of my work in the Senate. In terms of what I do,
it doesn't have any impact."

A curtain of silence descends for a moment in the van. Finally,
the same reporter quietly asks, "What would make it your 'time'
to run?"

Bill says mildly, "I'll know it if it's ever there. Right now I'm
interested [in]—and think about—being the best senator from
New Jersey and doing the best job I can. I've never been someone
who sits and wonders what he'll be doing in twenty years. I just
go ahead and do whatever the job is at hand and work as hard
as I can. If it happens, it happens."

N O O N : W I L D W O O D B O A R D W A L K   In front
of the information center, the mayor of Wildwood presents Bill
with an honorary lifeguard's sweatshirt. Afterwards, Bill tries his
hand at some of the games along the boardwalk. He uses a mallet
to try to catapult a rubber frog into a plastic flower. He misses.
He shoots a basketball toward a basket and misses that, too. On
the second try his touch returns, and the ball drops cleanly through
the hoop. Over lunch at a boardwalk restaurant, during which the
dieting Senator eats nothing, but watches several reporters wolf
down meatball grinders and slices of pizza, he answers even more
questions. Where does he stand on the B-1 bomber? "I oppose the
B-1." Has he gotten any Congressional appropriations lately for
the New Jersey shore? Well, yes, he has. He ticks off the amounts

At Wildwood, Bill was given an addition to his extensive sweatshirt collection. By law, as a senator, he must report on federal financial disclosure forms any gift he receives worth more than $100.00, and he cannot accept gifts worth more than $250.00. He borrowed change from a staffer to try this game. He missed.

on his fingers: $1 million for the Cape May National Wildlife Refuge, $700,000 for land purchase in the Pinelands, $930,000 for bathroom facilities and $600,000 for water wells at Sandy Hook, nearly $2 million to clean up floatable waste, and a good chance at obtaining monies to clean up various beaches. He finishes by mentioning appropriations he secured for a dune-grass planting project in Sea Isle City. "I take credit for every blade of grass," he says, smiling.

1 : 0 5   P . M .   T H E   V A N   Do you enjoy the world of politics? a reporter queries.

"I sure do," Bill says.

"Why?"

"Well, being in the Senate puts me in an environment where I have the opportunity to serve people and to hear people's stories. The combination of the two makes it rewarding for me. Being a senator is a tremendous opportunity to do things for people and to learn things. You've got to understand you're here as a senator because people want you here, and that their trust in you can be withdrawn at any time. Every day you have to feel you're contributing as a senator and growing personally. You're there only as long as people want you to be there."

"Why the Senate?" another reporter asks. "Why politics and not some other form of public service for you?"

Bill shrugs. "That's just the way I am." He twists around in his seat, looks the reporter straight in the eye. "You've got to understand yourself well enough to know what moves you," he murmurs.

1 : 1 5   P . M .   N O R T H   W I L D W O O D   When a little girl on the beach here shows Bill a hermit crab, Bill shouts into the shell, "Who's in there, huh? Who's in there?" sending the girl into a fit of happy giggles. When two high school boys invite Bill to try his hand at beach paddleball, he willingly does so, working the score to one–one before handing the paddle back and moving on. High school students seeking admission to the U.S. Naval Academy at Annapolis or the U.S. Military Academy at West Point must secure the sponsorship of one of their home state's senators. Farther along the beach, a middle-aged man clomps from the surf to pump Bill's hand and thank him for sponsoring the man's son as a candidate for admission to West Point.

"Did he get in?" Bill asks.

"He sure did!" the man crows.

Senators always try to get money included in the federal budget for projects in their home state. By pushing for federal funding for a dune-grass planting project in Sea Isle City, New Jersey, Bill helped save the dunes there from erosion. Such senatorial service is a source of great satisfaction to him.

Even senators can't always charm hermit crabs.

"Great!" Bill nods at the man's teenaged daughter standing nearby. "What about her? Annapolis?"

The girl's eyes register dread at the thought of entering a military school.

Bill flips a hand to show he's only teasing, and moves on. Along most of the beaches so far, the out-of-state tourists have outnumbered New Jerseyans about two to one, and, for Bill, the lack of his own constituents has been a source of mild frustration. To one reporter in the group, however, this same lack is uproariously funny. He has already told Bill that, as far as he's concerned, this whole beachwalk idea is nothing but a vote-getting stunt. Now every time Bill encounters an out-of-stater, the reporter, Zack [not his real name], brays with derisive laughter. Bill handles Zack's

At Hereford Lighthouse, Bill brightened one reporter's day.

scorn with good humor, but a few minutes later, at Hereford Lighthouse, he turns the tables on him. When the lighthouse's curator flips on an old signal light for Bill's inspection, Bill turns its beam on Zack. "Aha!" Bill's gesture seems to shout. "Now we've got you where we want you!" Everyone, including Zack, roars at the improvised joke.

A few stops later, Zack announces that he must leave the van and return to his newspaper. Bill, who has encountered more and more New Jerseyans throughout the afternoon, is noticeably more animated and talkative than at the start of the day. To him the important thing is not Zack's mocking laugh, it's hearing the thoughts and feelings of his constituents. "The strongest complaint I've heard is that the sun isn't out," he says. "That's pretty positive."

Now, in Avalon, as Zack prepares to depart from the van, Bill turns to him, and, spreading his arms, to the tune of "Hello, Dolly!" sings:

> *"Good-bye, Za-ack!*
> *Good-bye, Za-ack!*
> *It's been nice to have you here*
> *In our van!"*

After Zack's departure, the rest of the long afternoon seems more relaxed. At stops in Townsends Inlet, Sea Isle City, Strathmere, Peck Beach, Ocean City, and Longport, Bill seems to shrug off the dense heat while relishing his contact with humanity. At about five-thirty the sun breaks from behind milky clouds, bathing the sea and marshes in golden light. "We've got a beautiful sunset," says Bill. "A day with no sun ends with a beautiful sunset." Over the next two hours he will visit a home for the elderly, eat a salad for supper, play pickup basketball with some college kids on an outdoor court, and shake perhaps a hundred more hands. But the image right now of the land, sea, and sky seems to reflect in Bill's face as a chief reason he is traveling at all.

Everywhere Bill went, people sought him out for photographs . . .

. . . basketball . . .

. . . autographs . . .

. . . and hugs.

7:30 P.M. ATLANTIC CITY   In the lavender glow of the famous boardwalk, a reporter asks Bill whether he will be spending the night here or going home.

"Going home," he says.

"Isn't that inconvenient?"

"No. When I retired from pro basketball I swore that whenever I was in New Jersey I'd sleep at home. I'd rather get a quality sleep in my own bed than pay to sleep somewhere else."

On the way to his car, with seemingly as much energy as he had at the day's beginning, he says, "See you all tomorrow."

12

PATRIOTISM

THE DAY AFTER BILL Bradley finished his speech on flag burning he took it to his office and gave it to Marina Gentilini for retyping. The mood in the office was tense, everyone knowing that Bill would soon be speaking in the Senate and that his words could have repercussions for him far beyond the Senate chamber.

Shortly before nine-thirty, Bill boarded the Senate subway and not long thereafter entered the Senate chamber and strode to his desk in the back row.

Mornings in the Senate are usually given over to members' comments on various matters, and Bill's Democratic colleague John D. Rockefeller IV was winding up a speech saluting the 137th birthday of his home state, West Virginia. When Rockefeller finished, Bill raised his hand, and the presiding officer, Senator Herbert H. Kohl of Wisconsin, said, "The Chair recognizes the senator from New Jersey." Bill walked to a lectern located a few yards

Bill at Memorial Day ceremonies, Englewood, New Jersey

from the Senate well, unpocketed the speech, and clipped a small microphone to the breast pocket of his suit jacket. He gripped the lectern. Months later, he would not remember being nervous at this moment but totally focused on what he was about to say.

"MR. PRESIDENT," BILL ADDRESSED the presiding officer, "our American flag is best protected by preserving the freedom that it symbolizes. I cannot support a constitutional amendment that would limit that freedom. At the same time, I believe that anyone who burns the American flag is an ungrateful lowlife who fails to understand how special and unique our country is."

As Bill spoke, a Senate official reporter of debate stood nearby, using a portable stenographic machine to take down Bill's every word. Tape recorders are barred by Senate rules from use in the chamber. At the end of the reporter's ten-minute shift, his transcription would be fed into a computer that would organize Bill's words for printing in the day's *Congressional Digest*.

"Like most Americans," Bill continued, "I revere the flag as a symbol of our national unity. I want it protected from abuse. That is why I strongly supported a law to punish those who would destroy our flag. That is also why I regretted the Supreme Court's recent decision.* That is also why I enthusiastically support and today urge passage of another law that would make it illegal for someone to burn a flag if the act itself would incite violence.

"In our system, the first amendment† is what the Supreme Court at a particular time says it is. This court has said the flag-burning law violates freedom of expression. A future Supreme Court may reverse that decision. Although I wish the Supreme Court had ruled the other way, it did not. The question now is whether protecting the flag merits amending the Bill of Rights.

"In making the decision to oppose this amendment, I consulted my heart and my mind. My heart says to honor all those who died defending American liberty. My heart conjures up images of the Marines holding the flag on Iwo Jima, the crosses in the fields at Flanders, the faces of friends who never came back from Vietnam.

"My heart says, What a nation believes in, what it will preserve, what it will sacrifice for, fight for, die for, is rarely determined by words. Often people cannot express in language their feelings about many things. How do I know? Because I struggle with it every day.

---

* On June 11, 1990, the federal statute referred to here was ruled unconstitutional by the Supreme Court. Reason: the Court felt it violated the flag burner's constitutional right to freedom of expression. As stated here, Bill Bradley disagrees with the Court's decision, but he feels strongly that the Constitution should not be amended to outlaw flag burning, that the issue can be dealt with on a statutory level in a manner that is not unconstitutional.

† Here, Bill Bradley is referring to the first amendment in the Bill of Rights, the document protecting individual liberties that was added to the Constitution by our Founding Fathers in 1791. The first amendment guarantees for all individuals the freedoms of speech, press, religion, and assembly. As pointed out here, though, those rights are often subject to the Supreme Court's interpretation.

"Remember the pain you felt when the *Challenger* exploded before your eyes? Remember the joy you felt when World War II and the Korean War ended? Remember the shock you felt when you learned of the assassinations of President Kennedy and Martin Luther King? Remember the feelings of attachment you have for the Lincoln Memorial, the Statue of Liberty, the flag?

"These are symbols and shared memories for places, events, and things that tie us to our past, our country, and to each other, even when there are no words at all. When someone gives respect and recognition to them, we are moved, sometimes to tears. When someone demeans them or shows disrespect, we are outraged.

"My heart says, Honor the flag, and I do. My mind says, When our children ask why America is special among the nations of the world, we tell them about the clear, simple words of the Bill of Rights, about how Americans who won our independence believed that all people were blessed by nature and by God, with the freedom to worship and to express themselves as they pleased. We found these truths to be self-evident before any other nation in the world did, and even before we created the flag to symbolize them.

"Our Founding Fathers believed that fundamental to our democratic process was the unfettered expression of ideas. That is why the amendment that protects your right to express yourself freely is the first amendment, and politicians should never put that right at risk.

"Now if this constitutional amendment passes, we will have done something no Americans have ever done—amended the Bill of Rights to limit personal freedom.

"Even if you agree with the flag amendment, how can you know that the next amendment will be one you will like? You cannot. So let us not start. Once you begin chipping away, where does it stop? Do not risk long-term protection of personal freedom for a short-term political gain.

"America's moral fiber is strong. Flag burning is reprehensible, but our nation's character remains solid. My best judgment says

Official reporters of Senate debate use stenographic machines to record Senate proceedings in shorthand. So intense is the job that reporters are allowed to work only in ten-minute shifts, afterwards electronically feeding their transcriptions into a computer for printing in the *Congressional Record*.

we are in control of our destiny by what we do every day. We know the truth of Mrs. Bush's words that America's future will be determined more by what happens in your house than by what happens in the White House.

"I have traveled America for twenty-five years. I know we still have standards, insist on quality, believe in hard work, honesty, care about our families, have faith in God.

"A rapidly changing world looks to us to help them define for themselves what it means to be free. Our leadership depends more than ever on our example. This is the time to be confident enough in our values, conscientious enough in our actions, and proud enough in our spirit to condemn the antisocial acts of a few despicable jerks without narrowing our basic freedoms.

"My mind says that the best way to honor those who died to preserve our freedom is to protect those freedoms and then get on with the business of making America a better place.

"I took an oath to support and to defend the Constitution of the United States. Each senator has to decide in her own mind and in his own heart what he feels he must do to fulfill the promise he made to preserve and to stand by the Constitution. Different senators will arrive at different answers. For me, this amendment does not preserve the Constitution. To the contrary, it constricts, narrows, limits—makes it less than it was before. To preserve means to keep intact, to avoid decay, but this amendment would leave freedom of expression less intact, less robust, more in a state of decay. To support an amendment which would, for the first time in two hundred years, reduce the personal freedom that all Americans have been guaranteed by the Constitution would be, for me, inconsistent with my oath. I will never break my oath.

"Finally, I trust more the wisdom of the Founding Fathers in devising a system that guarantees liberty than I trust the posturing of today's politicians seeking to gain political advantage. In his dissenting opinion, Justice Stevens warned us about using the flag 'as a pretext for partisan dispute about meaner ends.' On one level, the debate about the flag amendment is not about the nature and limits of American symbols and American freedom; it is about pure politics. The purpose of this amendment, as the minority leader has admitted, is to provide a launching pad for vicious attacks on the integrity and patriotism of those who vote against it.

"The way it will begin is with an opponent saying, 'I will not question Senator X's patriotism, but I will question his judgment.' Let us be honest: the charge questions patriotism. Then comes the graphic thirty-second commercial featuring an unsavory, bearded lowlife burning a flag, and clearly implying that a particular senator is less than patriotic because he chose to preserve freedom over a constitutional amendment. This is sleazy politics, based on the ability to slur with impunity. A few years ago, the slur was directed at one's moral values, or commitment to family, or willingness to defend America. Now the same political poison aims for one's patriotism. Well, it makes me sick. A government or a politician who gains power by the slur will find little patience from the people and none from the opposite party when times get tough.

"Politics can be a mean business but it can also be a glorious business. Sometimes an event has unexpected consequences. Let's be frank: there is patriotism on both sides of this debate. So let me tell you what I believe about patriotism.

"Patriotism—I know how it feels to be proud to be an American. I remember how I felt back in 1964 when the United States Olympic Basketball Team defeated the Soviet Union in the finals. I remember standing on the victory stand with the gold medal around my neck, chills running up and down my spine, as the flag was raised and the national anthem played.

"I was proud to have won—for myself and for my country.

"Patriotism—it is like strength. If you have it, you do not need to wear it on your sleeve.

"The patriot is not the loudest one in praise of his country, or the one whose chest swells the most when the parade passes by, or the one who never admits we could do anything better.

"No, a patriot is one who is there when individual liberty is threatened from abroad, whether it is World War I, World War II, Korea, Vietnam, or even the wrongheaded action in Beirut in 1983—yes, that too. All those who served in these conflicts were defending liberty as our democracy chose, in its sometimes fallible way, to define the need to defend liberty.

"But you do not need a war to show your patriotism. Patriotism is often unpretentious greatness. A patriot goes to work every day to make America a better place—in schools, hospitals, farms, laboratories, factories, offices, all across this land. A patriot knows that a welfare worker should listen, a teacher should teach, a nurse should give comfort. A patriot accords respect and dignity to those he meets. A patriot tries, in a secular as well as a spiritual sense, to be 'his brother's keeper.'

"When the only grandfather I ever knew came to America, he went to work in a glass factory. He worked with his hands and he worked long and hard. After work he lived for three things: The first thing he lived for was going to the public library on a Saturday night to check out western novels, which he would read and reread over and over again. The second thing he lived for was to sit on his front porch on summer nights with a railroad whistle in the background and listen on the radio to his real love: baseball. And the third thing he lived for was to tell his grandson—me—what America meant to him. He said America was great because it was free and because people seemed to care about each other. Those two, freedom and caring, are the two inseparable halves of American patriotism. As Americans who love our flag, we must not sacrifice the substance of that freedom for its symbol, and we must learn to care more about each other.

"That is why I am in politics. And as long as I am in politics, I will not be stampeded by a handful of protestors whom I might despise or by a retinue of political consultants spreading the poison of today's partisan politics. Neither one represents the America I love and neither one will push me into restricting our fundamental freedom. To do so, I believe, would betray the meaning of the oath I took to support the Constitution and the promise I made to myself to always do what I thought was right.

"I oppose this amendment."

WITH THOSE WORDS, BILL unclipped the microphone and strode from the Senate chamber. He was relieved to have given the speech, but he wondered what effect it would have on his campaign for reelection.

By the next day, newspapers in New Jersey and elsewhere in the country were reporting Bill's opposition to the flag-burning amendment. His speech had effectively answered his campaign opponent's challenge on where he stood on the controversial issue. He had said what he had to say and said it clearly. Equally important, for the rest of the campaign nobody questioned Bill's patriotism.

13

CAMPAIGN: PART I

IN EARLY OCTOBER 1989 Bill Bradley's former Senate press secretary, Nick Donatiello, found himself working alone, daily, in a large modern office building on Route 9 in Woodbridge, New Jersey. The three-thousand-square-foot space contained no desks or chairs—just a telephone and an answering machine—and to Donatiello, who sat cross-legged on its vast carpeting, the silence and scarcity of furniture were emblematic. Only two years earlier he had been a business school graduate with a good job in a management consulting firm in San Francisco. Then Bill Bradley, whom he had met at Princeton while earning a bachelor's degree in engineering, had invited him to run his Senate press office in Washington. Though he had never worked in politics—indeed, hadn't the foggiest notion of what a Senate press office did—Nick eventually accepted Bill's offer. He proved to be an able press secretary, writing news releases and handling Bill's dealings with

The ballroom, Montclair State College, where Bill would announce his candidacy for a third term in the U.S. Senate

the Washington media. Soon Bill saw other potential in the big, bespectacled young man. In the spring of 1989 he asked Nick to be his campaign manager, overseeing all aspects of Bill's 1990 bid for Senate reelection. Once again, Nick pleaded ignorance of the job's requirements, but he soon said he'd do it. A few weeks later he attended a training session in Washington for novice managers like himself, sponsored by the Democratic Senatorial Campaign Committee. The session included lectures and seminars, and Nick gained from it two seemingly obvious but nevertheless valuable pieces of advice: First, a good campaign manager recognizes that every campaign is unique, meaning that what worked well in one campaign may not be relevant in another. Second, to be effective, a good campaign manager and his staff should always think.

Nick's first order of business in October had been to find the space that would serve as Bill's campaign headquarters. Having

Nick Donatiello in his office at Bill's Senate campaign headquarters in Woodbridge, New Jersey

done that, he next had to furnish it. Every day for almost a week he was on the phone to office suppliers, and before long, delivery trucks were rolling up outside the Woodbridge address with desks, chairs, lamps, filing cabinets, photocopiers, fax machines, and numerous other items in quantities sufficient to service a core staff that would eventually number twenty-five people. Perhaps the most important purchase, and one that Bill had specifically requested, was a computer system. This was, after all, the computer age, and Bill and his closest advisors felt that, in 1990, a campaign without a computer system needlessly hobbled itself. Over a period of months, Nick worked with several computer experts, equipping the office with a system that, for campaign purposes—mailings, record-keeping, and information storage—was very near state-of-the-art. Nick expected that Bill's opponent, whoever that turned out to be, would criticize the system's cost: a half million dollars.

But he also knew that this was going to be a sophisticated campaign, and he agreed with Bill that a computer, in this day and age, was essential.

While Nick toiled at equipping the office, other campaign staffers, led by finance director Betty Sapoch, one of his earliest campaign workers, were working at raising money to pay the campaign's many expenses—including equipment. They did this by mailing solicitations to Bill's earlier supporters and by organizing fund-raising events (usually dinners where Bill spoke) both in and out of New Jersey. By law, individual citizens can contribute only one thousand dollars per election to a candidate for federal office. But organizations of citizens known as political action committees, or PACs, can contribute as much as five thousand dollars per candidate per election, and a change in federal election laws in 1974 made the formation of new PACs relatively easy. From the mid 1970s, when there were roughly six hundred, the number of PACs had mushroomed. By 1988 there were more than four thousand, most representing special interests. PAC activities are controlled by the Federal Election Commission (FEC), which also monitors candidates' doings, and on the FEC rolls are PACs for bankers, lawyers, doctors, teachers, trash haulers, corporations, labor unions, and numerous other groups, each hoping to elect candidates who share their views. In fact, many PACs won't give money to a candidate unless he agrees with them on their pet issues. Bill and his fund-raising people would never make such promises. Bill's stance toward taking PAC money has always been that if a PAC wants to contribute to his campaign, fine—he considers the gesture a recognition of his work in the Senate. But beyond a "thank you" from him, the PAC should expect nothing in return. "Nobody gets anything for the money they give to Bill," one staffer said. "It just doesn't happen."

Bill's attitude toward PAC contributions also applies to those from individuals. In 1989, Michael Eisner, the head of Walt Disney Studios in California and one of Bill's longtime friends and staunch supporters, helped organize two big fund-raisers for Bill in Los Angeles. The events—a party and a catered dinner, both of which Bill attended—brought out the film industry's superstars and netted Bill's Senate campaign some eight hundred thousand dollars. Yet many political observers felt that the contributions—from stars like Goldie Hawn, Bill Cosby, and Robin Williams—were for Bill's eventual *presidential* campaign. No, said Bill, who gave his "Find your own Calcutta" speech at one of the fund-raisers, that's not how it's put to people. "We can't make people sign an oath when they give money that their motivation is to give it for Bill Bradley for U.S. Senate 1990," said a staffer, "although that's exactly who they're writing the check to. And they understand that. They've got to write it on the check." As for those whose contributions were ready only if Bill would tell them he was running for president, Bill would reply that if that was the case, "then don't make the contribution."

Whatever people's reasons for supporting Bill, they continued to flood his campaign with money. In an eight-month period from August '89 to April '90, he raised nearly three million dollars from donors in thirty-two states and the District of Columbia. Since his election in 1984 he had raised more than nine million dollars. As the coffers swelled, reporters began asking an obvious question: Why do you need so much money?

Bill usually answered by citing the high cost of buying television advertising in Philadelphia and New York City, the two major media markets for New Jersey. He would also mention not knowing who his opponent would be and what kind of campaign he or she would run. Would the opponent run a negative campaign, attacking Bill unfairly and forcing him to spend added campaign dollars on TV ads to defend himself? Already, in some political circles there was talk of the Republicans planning just such a campaign. "I like to be prepared," Bill said more than once. "In the age of slimeball politics you have to be ready for anything."

Bob McHugh reviewing Bill's TV spots

LIKE A CAREFULLY PLANNED expedition, the campaign for Bill's
Senate reelection took shape. In January, Bill instructed Nick to
hire a campaign press secretary, and Bill's top candidate for the
job was a former Associated Press reporter, Bob McHugh. Bill
had met McHugh in Washington when the reporter was covering
New Jersey politics there, and he liked McHugh's affable style of
professionalism. The thirty-eight-year-old McHugh was just ending a two-year stint as press secretary for retiring New Jersey
governor Thomas Kean, a Republican. Would he like to work for
Bill? Nick asked him.

He would, and in him, Nick would find an able colleague.
Months later the two men would find themselves serving as the
campaign's chief spokesmen—together answering the media's re-
lentless questions and doing so with patience and goodwill.

As the winter wore on, other campaign staffers came aboard. Greg Loder, a member of Bill's New Jersey staff, was hired as deputy campaign manager, responsible, in Bob McHugh's words, "for keeping the rest of the New Jersey Democratic leadership happy," and for overseeing voter registration drives and other fieldwork. Ken Shank, who played basketball at Princeton with Bill, agreed to be his old teammate's campaign treasurer, in charge of some nine million dollars. Greg McCarthy, a veteran of Bill's Washington press office, was brought up to Woodbridge to formulate Bill's daily campaign schedules, and Andrew Anselmi, a graduate student in political science, was hired to do research, particularly on Bill's yet-to-be-named opponent.

A whole branch of the campaign staff, under the direction of the campaign's comptroller, Jimmy Romanelli, was given over to dealing with federal election laws. Amendments to the Federal Election Campaign Act of 1972 require candidates for federal office to file periodic reports to the FEC. In addition, candidates for the U.S. Senate must register with and file campaign finance reports to the secretary of the Senate, while the Senate Ethics Committee has strict guidelines on how an incumbent senator can involve his Senate office with his campaign. For example, no monies from an incumbent's Senate budget can be used for campaign purposes, and only two members of an incumbent's Senate staff can perform political functions. While it is permissible for a Senator to send Senate-related mail for free under what is known as the franking privilege, it is unethical and illegal for a senator to frank his campaign mailings. Violating these laws and regulations can lead to a senator's prosecution by the U.S. Justice Department and to his censure and even expulsion by the U.S. Senate. Needless to say, Bill laid down to his staff a strict rule of his own: *We will obey the letter and the spirit of the law.* When Bob McHugh asked a staffer in Bill's Senate office to photocopy a news clipping for him, he was told that the office photocopier was unavailable for that purpose. When an envelope was mailed from Bill's Senate office to Woodbridge, a stamp was put on it. Romanelli and his staff spent days filling out even the simplest financial forms. After studying the campaign's file at the FEC, a reporter for the *Los Angeles Times* gushed to Bob McHugh: "You guys do things you don't even *have* to do!"

Meanwhile, the core campaign staff, including Marcia Aronoff from Bill's Senate office, Susan Thomases from New York City, and media consultant Michael Kaye from Los Angeles, were meeting as often as possible with Bill to crystallize the campaign's themes and strategies. Bill felt strongly that the campaign should stress his Senate record, and there was talk of sponsoring press events around New Jersey keyed to Bill's accomplishments. Bill also felt strongly that the chief themes of the campaign should be his commitment to children and the environment, and everyone agreed, given Bill's record on them, that the two issues formed a solid base from which to drive a campaign forward.

When should he announce his candidacy?

April, everyone agreed. April was two months before the Democratic primary, which would give the campaign time to see how its themes would play with the media and the public.

On April 2, 1990, Bill and his wife, Ernestine, entered a crowded ballroom on the campus of Montclair State College, where Ernestine teaches, and Bill spoke before the throng of well-wishers and reporters. "Today," he said, "I'm declaring my candidacy for reelection to the U.S. Senate."

"Yeah!" a man in the crowd shouted. Bill's next words were drowned by cheers and applause.

He told the assembly of his love for New Jersey, his passion for personal experience, and his efforts on behalf of the state's environment, particularly its shore. "I love my job because I can help people who have nowhere else to turn," he said. "I value my job because I can make a difference. . . . I enjoy my job because I can get to the bottom of things and make them right."

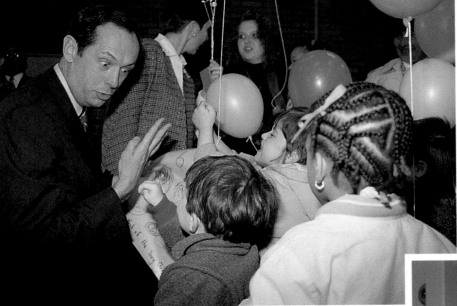

Saying hello to nursery school children who have come to hear Bill's speech

Bill and Ernestine enter the ballroom at Montclair State College to announce Bill's candidacy.

Announcing

He vowed to continue his fight against the tobacco lobby, which "rakes in a billion dollars a year from taxpayers to subsidize tobacco advertising," and he emphasized his commitment to children, including his own. The most important thing we can do, he said, is take care of our children, "and that begins with giving them what is most precious to us all—time. I think about that when I shoot a basketball with our daughter, or correct a spelling error. . . . When you think of it, our kids are the most important thing we can leave behind. . . .

"Maybe because I think our children are our most valuable assets, I have no tolerance for those who endanger them. For school bureaucrats who don't care about teaching, but only want a job —I say, fire them and pay the committed teachers more. For polluters who dump medical waste in our oceans and on our beaches—I say, slap fines on them until they go bankrupt. For corrupt officials who take money meant for housing or child nutrition and put it in their pocket—I say, throw them in jail. For drug kingpins who murder to make their millions off the destruction of a generation—I say, give them the death penalty."

To those who know Bill well, his closing words voiced a personal credo. "Each year I serve in the United States Senate, I respect the people of New Jersey more. Even amidst all the cynicism about politics and all the temptations to blame others, I never lose my enthusiasm and my commitment. I am fulfilled by my job representing the people of New Jersey, in all their diversity and with all their hopes.

"During the last year, I woke up more than once to news of people all over the world marching in the streets and some dying for what we have—a democratic process. At those moments I'm reminded that I'm part of a unique bond between the people and their elected leadership; I'm legitimized by the people. That's why being a U.S. senator for New Jersey is a special trust—a trust to which I give my clearest thought, my absolute integrity, and my maximum effort."

EVEN AS BILL SPOKE, it was clear that his chief rival for reelection would be Christine Todd Whitman, a forty-four-year-old former president of the state board of public utilities and a member of one of New Jersey's most prominent Republican families. The Republican strategy in choosing Christie Whitman seemed to be what Bill and his campaign staff had expected—to try to make Bill look bad. No one thought she could beat Bill. After all, he was extremely popular with New Jersey voters, having won the last election with 64 percent of the vote. Still, Republicans hoped she could deny him such a big victory this time and thereby tarnish his "presidential" luster.

Soon after accepting the Republican nomination, Whitman began her attacks. In stops around the state, she criticized the size of Bill's campaign war chest and called on him to spend no more than three million dollars. She argued that, since Bill was in favor of campaign finance reform (changing the way campaigns are funded and limiting campaign spending), he should voluntarily set an example. She also indirectly charged Bill with "testing the wind" before he took stands on issues. "I don't think he is as good as the aura that has built up around him," she said.

For his part, Bill continued to emphasize what he had done for his state's children and its environment and to justify his campaign money as a way of being prepared. "When you're not practicing, someone else is," read buttons that Bill's campaign staff distributed to supporters. The preparedness message, said Bob McHugh, applied equally to Bill's campaign fund.

Meanwhile, some newspapers thought Bill was pursuing a "politics of caution" in his campaign and cited the relative safeness of its themes. "Bradley, Though Popular, Chases Re-election on Tiptoe" read a headline in the May 30 issue of the *New York Times*. The same story described Whitman's spoiler role, suggesting that her real ambition lay in running for governor if she did well in this race.

Bill announced his candidacy twice—once in Montclair and once in
Camden, New Jersey. After announcing in Camden, Bill and Ernestine
toured a water treatment facility there.

Whatever their pursuits, Bill was not his state party's official
Senate candidate, nor was Christie Whitman hers, until they won
their party's separate primary elections on June 4. Meeting only
token opposition, Bill won the state Democratic primary easily;
running unopposed, Christie Whitman won hers. Thereafter, using
as her principal weapon a steady stream of press releases, Whitman

Republican Christie Todd Whitman would prove to be the toughest campaign opponent Bill ever faced.

intensified her campaign. Her main areas of contention with Bill as the summer progressed were:

1. Favoring an amendment outlawing flag burning. She questioned where Bill stood on the issue.

2. Continuing to insist that Bill's two positions on campaign spending and campaign finance reform didn't reconcile.

3. Accusing Bill of being "a coward and a sexist" because he wouldn't immediately agree to debate.

4. Demanding to know Bill's position on a $2.8 billion package of state tax increases pushed through the largely Democratic New Jersey legislature in June by Democratic Governor Jim Florio. Christie Whitman said she opposed the tax increases, as did most New Jerseyans. What about Bill? Where did he stand? she asked.

The first three issues were relatively easy to deal with, and Bill, along with Bob McHugh and Nick Donatiello, responded to them this way:

1. FLAG BURNING. In a June 20 speech on the Senate floor, Bill voiced his opposition to the flag burning amendment. That speech, which received statewide media attention, forever buried the subject as a campaign issue.

2. CAMPAIGN SPENDING AND CAMPAIGN FINANCE REFORM. Throughout the campaign, Bill repeated his belief in financial preparedness and said he favored campaign finance reform and hoped to see a measure passed during the 101st Congress. For now, though, he would play by the established rules.

3. COWARDICE AND SEXISM. Bill laughed when he heard the accusations. "We didn't have any problem with debating," said Bob McHugh. "We did get bogged down in a lot of campaign-to-campaign competitive stuff about when the debates were going to be held, who was going to sponsor them, that kind of thing. But we felt Bill was good enough on his feet that he wasn't going to embarrass himself." Nonetheless, throughout much of the summer—typically a quiet time for political campaigns—the "debate about debates" remained statewide news. When the two campaigns finally agreed in early September to hold two debates and two joint television appearances in October, the issue evaporated, although Christie Whitman complained that two debates weren't enough.

Of all issues in the campaign, the $2.8 billion Florio tax package was the only one that wouldn't go away. Whitman strategists knew that people throughout New Jersey were furious about the Florio tax increase. Christie Whitman's apparent strategy in raising it as an issue was to transfer some of that anger to Bill—the only

Bill's Senate campaign office in Woodbridge, New Jersey, gearing up for a fund-raising auction of items donated by such celebrities as Larry Bird, Dustin Hoffman, and Bruce Springsteen

available Democrat running statewide. One Whitman advisor called it "a hot button to push," and throughout the campaign Christie Whitman pushed it repeatedly.

The issue left Bill with an obvious dilemma. As one aide described Bill's options, "Do you dump on your fellow Democrat, Governor Florio? Or do you say you're in favor of the biggest tax increase in state history?"

Bill rejected both options, the first because Jim Florio was an old friend, one of Bill's earliest political supporters, the second because Bill was on record favoring "the lowest possible tax rate for the greatest number of Americans." He knew New Jersey residents despised the tax increase. "I hear your anger," he said at campaign stops. But he refused to exploit that anger for political purposes. Doing so, he felt, would be a form of demagoguery—rabble-rousing for political ends. Bill Bradley despised demagoguery. He was arguably one of the least demagogic members of the U.S. Senate.

Thus, instead of coming out either for or against the tax increase, Bill took what he felt was the only proper position: he chose not to discuss the issue at all. "I am a United States senator," he'd say, "and Florio's are state, not federal, tax increases. Governor Florio didn't call me up and ask my advice and counsel before he did the budget and tax package. We have different responsibilities. People ask me about Iraq—they don't ask Governor Florio."

In addition Bill pointed out that he didn't comment when Republican Governor Tom Kean raised taxes, and, as costly as it might be for him politically, he wasn't about to start now.

Bill's stance did not stop Whitman's forces from continuing their efforts to transfer voter anger from Florio to Bill. One fall day, a new Whitman bumper sticker began appearing on cars around the state. Its message defied logic, yet it summed up Christie Whitman's strategy perfectly.

The sticker said, "Get Florio—Dump Bradley."

As if the sticker weren't enough, for nearly the entire week of Bill's annual beachwalk it rained.

14

====

CAMPAIGN: PART II

FOR MICHAEL KAYE, BILL'S media consultant, the chief task that
summer of 1990 was filming the commercial spots that would be
aired on television later in the campaign. Throughout American
electoral history, candidates have vied for votes as if the electorate
were a pie comprised of various-sized slices. One slice typically
guaranteed a candidate contains his own party's "regulars," voters
who can be counted on in any election to "vote along party lines."
Another slice that candidates try to cut for themselves contains the
"crossover votes," voters of one party who "cross party lines" and
vote for the opposition candidate. Usually, though, the slice that
candidates compete for the most and whose size and leanings are
least easy to measure or predict contains the independents. These
middle-of-the-road voters, who resist easy labelling, tend to vote
for the person rather than the party, and often "split their ticket"
by voting for a mix of different candidates from either party. If

Bill campaigning at the Port Authority Bus Terminal in New York City with fellow U.S. senator Frank Lautenberg

enough independents vote the same way, they can sway the outcome of an election. Little wonder, then, that the battle for independent votes can gobble hefty chunks of a campaign's time and money.

Bill Bradley knew, and many studies had shown, that the most effective way to woo independent voters is through television ads. Thus, Bill called upon Michael Kaye to write and direct a group of ads that would attract this critical voting segment.

Kaye had been packaging Bill's TV spots since his first Senate campaign in 1978. A media consultant whose clients include Walt Disney Pictures, the trim five-foot-seven-inch Kaye was a diminutive contrast to his six-foot-five-inch client. Over the years, the two men had become close personal friends who liked to shoot

To attract independent voters, Bill hired his longtime friend and media consultant Michael Kaye to produce a number of television ads that emphasized his Senate accomplishments. The ads shown here are (*clockwise, from top left*): "Shoot, Shoot, Shoot," "Respite Care," "Beachwalk," and "Tough Decisions."

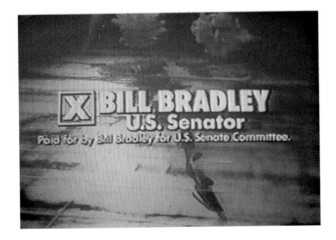

baskets together on election day. As Michael once said, "Bill is someone special to me."

To minimize production expenses, Michael hired a film crew from New Jersey, only flying in a director and a cameraman from California whom he had worked with on other productions. The first four ads were filmed in August 1990, when Bill was in New Jersey for his annual beachwalk. Straightforward, low-key, and emphasizing Bill's Senate accomplishments, the ads "totally reflect what Bill wants to talk about," Michael said. The first, on the theme of Bill's commitment to children, showed Bill in a school gym addressing a group of youngsters while his voice-over emphasized the millions of dollars he has legislated for the health and education of New Jersey's kids. "Shoot! shoot! shoot!" the kids shout when someone tosses Bill a basketball. Bill shoots— and the ball swishes cleanly through the basket.

Spot Number Two, depicting Bill alone late at night in his Washington office (the spot was actually filmed in Woodbridge), is meant to emphasize Bill's ability to make tough decisions. "When Bill Bradley voted against the tax bill that's caused our huge budget deficit, he didn't have much company . . . ," said a voice-over. "And when Senator Bradley voted against giving tax breaks to savings and loan speculators he stood alone. . . . Sometimes you have to stand alone." (Close with Bill walking solo to his car in an empty parking lot.)

Spot Number Three was aimed at a specific program, respite care, that Bill pushed through the Senate. A woman appearing on-screen says that without respite care, "we could no longer keep my ailing mother with us at home. . . . We now have someone to sit with her for a few hours so that we can go to the park together or watch our children play ball. . . . Having my mother with us at home is a blessing for which we will always be grateful to Senator Bradley."

Spot Number Four showed Bill greeting people along the Jersey shore while his voice-over said, "It's my way of saying that I care about them and I care about the shore. . . . I'll never stop fighting the dumpers and polluters who, left unchecked, would destroy our beaches and oceans." Bill (on a beach, facing the camera): "You've got my word on it."

Michael filmed several other spots. One, aiming at humor, had Bill cite the travails of being a senator and ended with him putting his feet on his desk to reveal them shod in basketball sneakers. Others, readied in case the campaign got rough, attacked Christie Whitman's record on taxes while she was a freeholder (commissioner) from Somerset County.

No one on Bill's campaign staff doubted the need for the negative ads. But neither did they feel the campaign was in serious difficulty. As late as October 22, newspaper polls around New Jersey would show Bill with roughly a two-to-one lead over Christie Whitman. The positive ads emphasizing Bill's record seemed just the right vehicles for attracting and holding independents and ultimately driving the campaign to victory.

BILL AND HIS STAFF also developed a more innovative ad, one never seen before in a campaign. Nick Donatiello called it "the eight hundred number political commercial," and its idea was to spotlight an issue and invite viewers to comment on it by phoning an 800 number. Viewers were free to express their views, and, in return for calling, Bill's staff sent them a brochure on the topic, in this case, protecting children from lead poisoning. "The great thing about Bill Bradley," said Nick, "is he's open to new ideas. We learned a lot through the lead commercial. Literally thousands of people called with comments ranging from 'This is great, we love what you're doing' to 'Would you run for president' to 'I'm really glad someone cares about this' to negative comments, highly technical questions, and environmental concerns. Bill always wants to hear what people think, and the ad proved to be a new way for him to listen to people."

DESPITE HIS CAMPAIGN'S SOPHISTICATED activities, the part of it Bill still liked most was the more old-fashioned business of wading into crowds and meeting people. Originally, plans called for Bill to be up in New Jersey making campaign stops from October 5, when Congress was expected to adjourn for the year, to election day on November 6. Unfortunately, those plans collapsed when Congress couldn't pass a budget.

On January 29, 1990, President Bush had sent his $1.2 trillion budget for fiscal year 1991 to Congress for its approval. Throughout the spring and summer, and continuing through October, Congress and President Bush disagreed on a spending package that would meet the federal government's spending needs while simultaneously reducing the annual deficit. In 1988, George Bush had campaigned for the presidency and won on a pledge of no new taxes—the famous "Read my lips" pledge. On June 26, 1990, he found himself backpedaling from that pledge, recognizing that taxes would have to be raised, that different spending programs would have to be trimmed and some cut altogether. But which ones? The budget battle was just like one of Bill's student leadership seminars, only for real, and instead of taking place in a college classroom, it was unfolding on Capitol Hill before the entire nation.

Night after night, what the nation saw on its television screens and in its newspapers was a Congress unable to pass a budget. On September 30, when the government theoretically ran out of the money budgeted for 1990, Congress passed something called a continuing resolution to keep the government running through October 5. When that date came and still no budget had been passed, however, President Bush vetoed another continuing resolution, effectively shutting down the government. Regular government employees—office workers, guards, custodians, and others—could not report to work because there was no longer money budgeted to pay them. News broadcasts showed tourists encountering "Closed" signs at the Washington Monument, the Statue of Liberty, and other government facilities. Only when the House of Representatives made a degree of progress in budget talks did President Bush resume signing continuing resolutions, and the government reopened. By then, though, the damage had been done. Not only could Bill Bradley and other incumbent senators and congressmen not return to their home states to campaign, but an "anti-incumbent" mood began growing across the country. Voters derided Congress's inability to pass a budget and, worse, resented the prospect of higher federal taxes. Seventy-one percent of voters questioned in a *Wall Street Journal*/NBC poll published on October 26 disapproved of Congress's handling of the budget. In a year when Congress had voted itself a pay raise, when five senators were being investigated for using their offices improperly, when a congressman was about to resign for sexual misconduct, and when taxpayers were faced with a five-hundred-million-dollar bailout of the nation's savings and loan corporations, the budget stalemate further fueled the "throw the rascals out" mentality.

In New Jersey, some voters wished Bill would take a more visible role in the budget talks, particularly regarding tax fairness, an issue that Bill had championed in 1986. But this time Bill took a more behind-the-scenes role in budget negotiations, successfully blocking measures that would have made taxes less fair, and actually voting against the budget package when it was finalized because of the harm he felt it would bring to middle-class taxpayers and to social programs he favored.

A budget that Bill voted against was finally passed on the evening of October 27. At 1:17 on the morning of October 28, a tired 101st Congress finally adjourned. Though he had managed to get back to New Jersey for a few campaign functions in October, Bill had essentially lost three weeks of campaign time. Everyone in his camp was frustrated. "It's kind of like we've had a big party

The first Bradley-Whitman debate, on domestic issues, was televised from Secaucus, New Jersey.

planned," said Bob McHugh, "but the guest of honor hasn't been able to make it."

TWO FUNCTIONS BILL DID make in mid-October were the debates with Christine Whitman. American political debates date back to the early nineteenth century, when opponents for public office spoke for hours before huge gatherings on the day's issues. In modern times the importance of debates was less clear until 1960, when Richard M. Nixon and John F. Kennedy became the first candidates for the presidency to debate each other on national television. Entering the debate, Kennedy was trailing in the polls, but his forceful, photogenic presence carried the day and, many felt, won him the presidency.

The conventional wisdom was that an incumbent had everything to lose, a challenger everything to gain by debating. Indeed, one slip of the tongue by the incumbent or one memorable line delivered by the challenger could cost an incumbent votes. Bill

Bradley knew the conventional wisdom. But he was not afraid to
debate, having done so twenty-three times in his Senate election
in 1978.

The first debate, scheduled for Sunday, October 14, would be
limited to domestic issues. As the date approached, Bill made extra
time in his Senate schedule to review his position on different
topics and to consider the likely points his challenger would make.
He wrote opening and closing statements and essentially memo-
rized them. He honed his debating technique through practice
debates with his closest advisors.

The hour-long debate was held in a television studio in Secaucus, New Jersey. Beforehand, a studio assistant daubed Bill's
face with pancake makeup to soften its shadows, and a technician
clipped a microphone to each candidate's lapel. For the photographers present, the two candidates shook hands. Then, as a crowd
of about one hundred in the studio breathlessly watched, the televised debate began.

As Bill expected, Christie Whitman used her opening statement
to step up her attacks on him. "I'm in this race because I don't
think New Jersey can afford a part-time senator with one eye on
the White House," she said. "I don't think we can afford a senator
who lacks the political courage to take a stand on the Florio tax
plan. And I know we can't afford a Congress that spends more
on itself than we do on drug treatment. I want to be a leader for
New Jersey, and, strange and simple as it sounds, leadership requires taking a lead. Leadership is not [spending] five hundred
thousand dollars in public opinion polls and then not having a
public opinion on the Florio tax program. Leadership is not saying
that balanced budget amendments and a line item veto are gim-
micks and not offering anything in their place. Leadership is not
taking two hundred and twenty thousand dollars in backdoor
speaking fees and then voting to ban the practice. And leadership
isn't refusing to give back money from an indicted savings and
loan official when many of your compatriots are giving back all

of their savings and loan money. And finally, leadership isn't talking about children's futures and refusing to do anything about
Congress's spending that robs from all our futures. I think this
election is a choice between someone who's become part of the
status quo and business as usual, and someone who's dedicated to
change. Throughout the campaign I've gone the extra mile. I'm
waiting for Bill Bradley to take the first step."

Bill, for his part, held to his campaign strategy and stressed
his considerable accomplishments. "On election night six years ago
I made some promises to the people of New Jersey," he said. "I
promised to fight for more money and stronger laws to clean up
toxic wastes. Look at the record: we have a new superfund. I
promised I'd fight for a new federal income tax, one with lower
rates and fewer loopholes—a fairer system. Look at the record: I
got tax reform done. I promised I'd fight for laws that allow the
elderly to stay at home with their families instead of being pushed
into nursing homes. Look at the record: I got the law passed. I
promised to protect drinking water. Look at the record: I got the
money to clean up contaminated wells in Camden.

"I've kept my promises for the children of New Jersey. Look
at the record: I've gotten millions of dollars to improve their health
and education. Above all, I think I've tried to be an independent-
minded senator, one that didn't put a finger in the air to see which
way the wind was blowing, but one who used his judgment, took
some risks, in order to stand up for what he believed was right."

The debate itself was more like a glorified press conference.
A panel of four reporters would ask a question of one candidate,
who had ninety seconds to respond, and then the other candidate
had a minute's rebuttal time.

Not surprisingly, given the tenor of the times, many of the
reporters' questions were on budgets and taxes. When a reporter
cited a poll that said three out of four New Jersey voters wanted
to know Bill's thoughts on Florio's tax plan, Bill repeated his
position: he was not going to exploit the issue for political purposes.

Said Whitman in her rebuttal: "I find it outrageous . . . to say it's political pandering to respond to what the people of New Jersey are asking."

When Christie Whitman was asked what combination of program cuts and tax increases she would support to reduce the deficit, she said she favored keeping federal spending at current levels. She said that budget reform could come 1) if Congress allowed a line-item veto, giving a president the right to cut individual items from the federal budget,* and 2) if Congress created a balanced-budget amendment to the Constitution, which would require a balanced budget every year.

Bill felt that keeping the budget at current levels was an inadequate response to the deficit problem—and to the reporter's question. He counterattacked, listing $140 billion in budget cuts he would make and $95 billion in revenues he would raise by closing corporate loopholes and taxing pollution. We don't need to amend the Constitution in order to balance the budget, he argued. And as for the line-item veto, it's nothing but a "political gimmick" that would be bad for the people of New Jersey because it would allow the president to cut specific monies allocated for the state. "If you're interested in running for the United States Senate," Bill concluded, "you've got to make the decisions. You can't simply campaign on slogans."

Through questions on campaign finance, abortion, sludge, media consultants, Supreme Court appointments, and the limitation of congressional terms, the debate continued. But was anybody listening? The TV station estimated that nearly six hundred thousand New Jerseyans were settled in front of their TV sets, watching the debate, but as they watched did they understand what Bill had accomplished for them? Or—and this was any incumbent's nightmare—was Christie Whitman succeeding in making them forget what Bill had achieved on their behalf, thereby turning him into just

---

* Under the Constitution, the president can only accept or veto the budget in its entirety.

In the second debate, Bill's deep understanding of foreign policy matters shone through.

another politician? In his essay on George Washington, the New Jersey poet William Carlos Williams called the Father of our Country "the typical sacrifice to the mob," and, in a way, that was what Whitman was trying to make Bill ("Get Florio, Dump Bradley"). She had been recruited by the Republicans to try to hurt Bill politically, and by hectoring him on the Florio tax issue and calling him names ("part of the status quo"), she could say she was only doing her job. Making things miserable for Bill. Pushing the hot button.

EVEN IN THE SECOND debate, which was supposed to be on foreign policy, Christie Whitman sneaked in the issue of Florio's tax increase. It was October 23, a rainy night exactly two weeks before the election. Polls around New Jersey still showed Bill with roughly a two-to-one lead, but the number of undecided voters in some polls was troubling. For example, in a poll of four hundred voters in central New Jersey's Somerset County conducted by its newspaper, the *Courier-News*, 44.2 percent favored Bill, and 27 percent favored Whitman, but 26 percent were undecided (2.8 percent refused to answer). With the strong anti-incumbency mood on the winds, a vote against Bill by the undecideds was not impossible. If such a vote happened statewide, he could lose the election.

Greeting well-wishers with Ernestine outside the chandeliered ballroom of the swank Birchwood Manor in Whippany, where the second debate would be held, Bill knew he had to do well. Fortunately he had years of foreign policy study under his belt, and his grasp of recent foreign events was firm and supple. He answered questions about Iraq's August 2 invasion of Kuwait by saying he supported President Bush's sending U.S. forces to defend Saudi Arabia, but criticized the administration for not warning Iraq against invasion in the first place. He further faulted the president for not releasing some of our strategic petroleum reserves, which Bill had fought years ago to put in place, to offset higher oil prices. On those and other points, Christie Whitman did not substantially disagree with him.

The biggest disagreement of the evening arose over a recent U.S. vote in the United Nations condemning Israel for killing twenty-one Palestinians during a rock-throwing incident in Jerusalem on October 8. Whitman, who had driven that morning to the Saddle River home of Richard Nixon for a two-hour briefing on foreign policy matters with the former president, felt that the U.S. did the right thing in condemning the Israelis for the killings. Bill disagreed. "I don't think the facts were clear," he said. "There could very well have been provocation. I also don't agree with Mrs. Whitman that the Palestinian-Israeli issue is totally separate from what happened in the Persian Gulf. In fact, one could argue [it] could have been a provocation . . . fomented by Saddam Hussein . . . to break up [our] Arab alliance . . . in the Persian Gulf." Her response, he concluded, "indicates a rather superficial view" of the Middle East.

On other questions, Bill's answers were crisp and succinct. On money to recently liberated Eastern Europe: "We have to make

Because Congress recessed so late, Bill had little more than a week to actively campaign. At a pharmaceutical plant in central New Jersey, he encountered both supportive and anti-incumbency feelings.

a bigger effort over there if our rhetoric about democracy and freedom means anything." On economic aid to the Soviet Union: "The only way the Soviet Union can move into the twenty-first century is to have an open society that dramatically cuts its defense budget and that takes radical reform measures to move it to a market economy. Only *they* can do that. *We* can't do that." He chose to fight fire with fire by attacking Whitman for supporting "gold-plated weapons systems" when there are other systems that can do the job at one-tenth the cost, and for favoring a constitutional balanced budget but not saying how she would do the balancing. In his closing remarks he said, "Nobody knows what's going to happen in the next six years. So, ultimately this is a race

This was the part of campaigning that Bill Bradley loved. Still, there was no telling how close the election would be.

about whose judgment the people trust and who they want making what could be life-and-death decisions about their future."

Christie Whitman's closing remarks were a reiteration of the anti-incumbent themes she had hammered at for months:

"We cannot condone a Congress that is failing democracy. . . .

"We are being let down by our congressional leadership, Bill Bradley included. . . .

"I support a balanced budget law to force limits on government spending. . . .

"I'll propose an amendment to cut Congress's own two-billion-dollar budget. . . .

"I'll support a limit on terms of office. . . .

"My opponent is one of the best examples of how twelve years in Washington can change well-intentioned people into status quo politicians. . . .

"As much as we have witnessed a revolution of freedom across this world, we need a revolution in Congress."

Bill had spoken well throughout the debate, but the applause that greeted Christie Whitman's remarks was another sign that she might be making headway.

THE QUESTION WAS, HOW much?

Since early summer more than a million New Jerseyans had joined a grass-roots group called Hands Across New Jersey to protest Governor Florio's tax hike. Were these angry citizens being swayed by Christie Whitman's message to get Florio by voting against Bill?

To try to answer such questions, Bill maintained the services of a private polling firm in Connecticut run by a close friend, Joe Peretz. "Most of our polling," said Nick Donatiello, "is to see what people care about, because part of being a senator is responding to people's concerns." But Peretz could also conduct polls to track voter leanings, and that is what he had been doing throughout the campaign. On October 26, Peretz conducted his last poll for Bill before the election. Pollers phoned hundreds of registered voters across the state, asking them, if the election were held today, which candidate they would vote for. Their findings: 58 percent said they would vote for Bill, compared with 64 percent in 1984. According to those numbers, Bill's lead had slipped but was still secure.

And yet polls that would not surface until after the election painted a more disturbing picture. A poll by the Eagleton Institute of Politics at Rutgers University conducted a week before November 6 showed Bill leading by 26 percentage points among voters in general, *but by only 2 percentage points among voters who considered themselves very interested in the Senate race*. Two percentage points! A 2-percent lead! The institute's numbers also showed that 76 percent of those polled felt that the Florio tax hike was an issue in the Senate race. As unfair as it might seem to Bill's supporters, the Republican strategy of linking him to Florio was working brilliantly.

Unfortunately, by an oversight at the institute, those poll results were not released. Yet even if they had been, it was too late for Bill and his campaign staff to change strategy. The election was seven days away. Bill was not about to dishonor himself by discussing what he had vowed not to discuss. The die was cast. In the last two weeks of the campaign he did order his negative TV ads to be aired to counter his opponent's negative radio ads. But, all in all, he had to live with the course he had set.

In sports bars, bowling alleys, firehouses, street corners, office buildings, factories, shopping malls, and parks, Bill sensed that voter anger at Governor Florio and Congress was turning toward him. His staff had rented a newer car in place of the Oldsmobile Cutlass that had 160,000 miles on its odometer and whose spaciousness Bill loved. The new car, typical of modern sedans, fit Bill like a sardine can. After less than a day in it, Bill ordered his driver, Hugh Drummond, to tape sponges on the dashboard to cushion his knees. In the campaign's last week, with Bob McHugh and Michael Kaye in the back seat and a can of cashews at his knees for nourishment, Bill made stops in every one of New Jersey's twenty-one counties. He shook hands, said, "I need your support on Tuesday," and listened to his constituents' fear and anger.

Perhaps nowhere was there a better microcosm of voters' feelings than in Manhattan's bustling Port Authority Bus Terminal the night before the election. For nearly three hours there Bill, taking deep breaths to stave off fatigue, shook hands with hundreds of New Jersey commuters as they rushed to their evening buses. At one point he was joined by his fellow senator Frank Lautenberg, who shouted, "I'm Senator Lautenberg! Vote for Bill Bradley! He deserves your vote tomorrow! Say hello to Bill!" Many people told Bill they'd support him the next day, but several said they wouldn't. One woman said, "I voted for you six years ago but not this time. I'm not voting for any incumbent."

One man said, "None o' you guys works for a living. Me, I go to work every day. What do you do? Go back to Washington."

Another man said, "I make thirty-eight thousand a year. By the time I finish payin' state and federal taxes I got nothin'. And now you guys go and raise my taxes?"

Bill, trying to get a word in edgewise, said, "In 1986 I got a tax reform act passed that saved the people of New Jersey a billion dollars a year in federal taxes."

The man was too angry to listen. Bill's right hand was swollen and red from shaking hands. As the man complained about the high cost of living in New Jersey, Bill kept murmuring, "I hear you."

Standing nearby, Michael Kaye said, "At any campaign stop you expect to hear some negatives. The people I'm worried about are the ones not saying anything at all."

15

ELECTION

When the polls closed at seven-thirty the following night, Bill found himself in the tightest election battle of his life. In the ballroom of the Meadowlands Hilton in Secaucus, where he had claimed victory six years earlier, anxious friends and staffers watched three banks of television monitors as grim-faced anchormen from stations around the region delivered the shocking news: with 43 percent of New Jersey's precincts reporting, Christie Whitman was leading by three thousand votes!

"I'm going to walk around," said Bill's soft-spoken driver, Hugh Drummond.

In a twelfth-floor suite, with his family and a few close staffers, Bill watched the results, feeling concern but not surprise. His talks with voters in the campaign's last eight days had convinced him it was going to be a close contest. At eight o'clock that bright, windy morning, after having voted with Ernestine at Morris Cath-

Bill and Ernestine arriving at Morris Catholic High School in Denville to vote

olic High School in Denville, he had answered a reporter's question about the election's outcome by saying, "In basketball, if you win by one basket you still win. In an election, if you win by one vote it's still a win and you take it."

But to be losing?

It wasn't over yet, he knew. Most of the precincts reporting were in rural western New Jersey, a long-standing Republican stronghold. As he had seen in 1984, the largely urban and suburban eastern counties, where he had always done well, tended to report their votes much later.

Still, the mood in the ballroom was tense. Television reporters in the middle of the floor called the closeness of the race shocking. Voter outrage at Florio's taxes, Congress's paralysis, and Bill's own cautious campaign were probably factors in making the race tight, they said. Bill's outspending his opponent in the campaign ten to

As the networks began reporting a tight Senate race in New Jersey, the mood at the Meadowlands Hilton was grim.

one had not helped him at the polls, they added. On television, a Cable News Network anchor said, "This is certainly the shocker of the evening so far!"

Bill was not the only incumbent feeling voters' wrath. In North Carolina, Georgia, Vermont, Minnesota, and other states, congressmen and senators found themselves either holding on to their offices for dear life or actually losing.

Could Bill lose? his supporters silently wondered.

"We're gonna win," said a confident Hugh Drummond, re-entering the ballroom. "It's just gonna take a little longer."

He was right. As precincts in eastern New Jersey began to weigh in, the tide began to turn. With 50 percent of the votes reported, Christie Whitman had 506,829, but Bill had 507,229. He had recaptured the lead!

A cheer went up around the ballroom. As more reports came in, Bill began to inch away. With 53 percent of the votes reported, Bill had 516,744 votes to Whitman's 512,909. With 58 percent tallied, Bill had 572,236 to Whitman's 563,271. At 10:05 Eastern Standard Time, CBS News said that, based on its polling projections, Bill Bradley was the winner in his race for U.S. Senator. The cheer that erupted from the crowd was loud and sustained. Over the next twenty minutes NBC and Cable News Network agreed with CBS's projection, and by eleven P.M. a sadly smiling Christie Whitman, wistful but pleased with her remarkable showing, conceded defeat.

Everyone in the room was visibly relieved. A rock 'n' roll band hired for the evening launched into a torrid version of "Roll Over, Beethoven," and staffers and supporters took to the dance floor and shook. Bill's Senate press secretary, Michael Jones, shouted, "We won! That's what's important!"

But that wasn't all that was important. From the close victory, Bill learned that voters' distrust of politicians in general runs deep. "They don't believe we talk honestly with them," he told a news columnist later, "and too often they're right." He was not one to be a Monday-morning quarterback, but he would admit later that his campaign themes should have been stronger and more clearly stated. "People want politicians to talk about issues that affect their lives," he said. By their close vote people were telling him to "continue to respect us, listen to us, work for us." The agony for Bill was "there are things affecting their lives, some of which I don't have any control over."

Nonetheless, in the future, though he considered himself a good listener, he would work to listen more. Though associates described him as a tireless legislator, he would try to work even more tirelessly to legislate on his constituents' behalf. Though excellence had always been a personal pursuit of his, he would

11:00 P.M. Stephanie, Ernestine, Bill, and Theresa Anne receiving the plaudits of Bill's supporters. A long and difficult campaign had made Bill a better public servant.

take greater risks to ensure that excellence was achieved. In 1990, Bill had learned that you can be an outstanding senator, as he had become, but, in your constituents' eyes, no matter how much good you have done, you can do more.

Even an outstanding United States senator can never be good enough.

IN THE PACKED HOTEL ballroom, Bill stood on the stage arm in arm with Ernestine, her daughter Stephanie, and Theresa Anne as people applauded and cheered him. A few moments earlier he had told the throng that he understood voters' frustrations with their elected officials and their government. "I get the message," he said. "I hear you, I really do." He vowed he would "work to tax things we don't like, such as pollution. I'll continue to work for better health care and for kids; I'll continue to work for the environment."

For Bill it had been a difficult campaign in a difficult political climate. It had made him a better public servant.

A SPEECH

FROM A FLOOR STATEMENT BY
SENATOR BILL BRADLEY
ON RACE AND CIVIL RIGHTS,
JULY 10, 1991

Dear Mr. President,

In 1988 you used the Willie Horton ad to divide white and black voters and appeal to fear. Now, based on your remarks about the 1991 Civil Rights Bill, you have begun to do the same thing again. Mr. President, we implore you—don't go down that path again. It's not good for the country. We can do better.

Racial tension is too dangerous to exploit and too important to ignore. America yearns for straight talk about race, but instead we get code words and a grasping after an early advantage in the

1992 election. Continued progress . . . requires moral leadership and a clear-sighted understanding of our national self-interest. And that must start with our president.

So, Mr. President, tell us how you have worked through the issue of race in your own life. I don't mean speech-writer abstractions about equality or liberty but your own life experiences. When did you realize there was a difference between the lives of black people and the lives of white people in America? Where did you ever experience or see discrimination? How did you feel? What did you do? What images remain in your memory? Tell us more about how you grappled with the moral imperatives embodied in race relations and how you clarified the moral ambiguities that necessarily are a part of the attitude of every American who has given it any thought—any thought at all.

Do you believe silence will muffle the gunshots of rising racial violence in our cities? Do you believe that brotherhood will be destroyed by candor about the obstacles to its realization? Do you believe ignoring the division between the races will heal it? If you truly want it healed, why don't you spend some of your political capital represented by your 70 percent approval ratings and try to move our glacial collective humanity one inch forward?

Mr. President, you say you're against discrimination. Why not make a morally unambiguous statement and then back it up with action? At West Point you said you "will strike at discrimination wherever it exists." How will you do that and when? Why not try to change the racist attitudes of some Americans—even if they voted for you—so that all Americans can realize our ideals?

Mr. President, if these concerns are wrong, please dispel them. Please explain the following bases for our doubt.

DOUBT ONE: Your record. Back in 1964 you ran for the Senate and you opposed the Civil Rights Act of that year. Why?

I remember that summer. I was a student intern in Washington, D.C., between my junior and senior years in college, and I was in this Senate chamber that hot summer night when the bill passed.

I remember the roll call. I remember thinking, America is a better place because of this bill. All Americans—white or black—are better off. I remember the presidential election that summer, too, when Senator Goldwater made the Civil Rights Act an issue in his campaign. I came to Washington that summer as a Republican. I left as a Democrat.

Why did you oppose that bill? Why did you say that the 1964 Civil Rights Act, in your words, "violates the constitutional rights of all people?" Remember how many parts of our country functioned before it was passed? Separate rest rooms and drinking fountains for black and white, blacks turned away from hotels, restaurants, movies. Did you believe that black Americans should eat at the kitchen steps of restaurants, not in the dining room? Whose constitutional rights were being violated there?

Were you just opposing the Civil Rights Bill for political purposes? Were you just using race to get votes?

Did you ever change your mind and regret your opposition to the Civil Rights Act? If so, when? Did you ever express your regret publicly? What is your regret?

When you say today that you're against discrimination, I don't know what you mean, because you have never repudiated or explained your past opposition to the most basic widening of opportunity for black Americans in the twentieth century, the Civil Rights Act of 1964.

It sounds like you're trying to have it both ways—lip service to equality and political maneuvering against it.

What does your record mean? What have you stood for?

DOUBT TWO: Economic reality. Mr. President, over the last eleven years of Republican rule the poor and the middle class in America have not fared well. The average middle-income family earned $31,000 in 1977 and $31,000 in 1990. No improvement. During the same time period the richest 1 percent of American families went from earning $280,000 in 1977 to $549,000 in 1990. Now, how could that have happened? How could the majority of voters have supported governments whose primary achievement was to make the rich richer? The answer lies in the strategy and tactics of recent political campaigns.

Just as middle-class America began to see their economic interests clearly and to come home to the Democratic Party, Republicans interjected race into campaigns, to play on new fears and old prejudices, to drive a wedge through the middle class, to pry off a large enough portion to win.

Mr. President, most Americans recognize that in economic policy Republicans usually try to reward the rich, and Democrats usually don't. I accept that as part of the lore and debate and rhythm of American politics. What I can't accept, because it eats at the core of our society, is inflaming racial tension to perpetuate power and then using that power to reward the rich and ignore the poor. It is a reasonable argument over means to say more for the wealthy is a price we pay to "lift all boats." It is a cynical manipulation to send messages to white working people that they have more in common with the wealthy than with the black worker next to them on the line, taking the same physical risks and struggling to make ends meet with the same pay.

Mr. President, I detest anyone who uses that tactic—whether it is a Democrat like George Wallace or a Republican like David Duke. The irony is that most of the people who voted for George Wallace or David Duke or George Bush because of race haven't benefited economically from the last decade. Many of them are worse off. Many have lost jobs, health insurance, pension benefits. Many more can't buy a house or pay property taxes or hope to send their child to college. The people who have benefited come from the wealthiest class in America. So, Mr. President, put bluntly, why shouldn't we doubt your commitment to racial justice and fair play when we see who has benefited most from the power that has been acquired through sowing the seeds of racial division?

DOUBT THREE: Your inconsistent words. Most Americans who have absorbed our history know the wisdom of Zora Neale

Hurston's words: "Race is an explosive on the tongues of men." Race is most especially an explosive on the president's tongue—or the tongues of his men.

We need to be led not manipulated. We need leadership that will summon the best in us, not the worst. . . . Yet you have tried to turn the Willie Horton code of 1988 into the quotas code of 1992. You have said that's not what you're doing, but, as you said at West Point, "You can't put a sign on a pig and say it's a horse."

Why do you say one thing with your statement against discrimination and another with your opposition to American businesses working with civil rights groups to get a civil rights bill most Americans could be proud of? Are you sending mixed signals or giving a big wink to a pocket of the electorate?

We measure our leader by what he says and by what he does. If both what he says and what he does are destructive of racial harmony, we must conclude that he wants to destroy racial harmony. If what he says and what he does are different, then what he does is more important. If he says different things at different times that are mutually contradictory, then we conclude he's trying to pull the wool over someone's eyes.

Mr. President, you need to be clearer so that people on all sides understand . . . what you believe and how you propose to make those beliefs a reality. Until then, you must understand that an increasing number of Americans will assume your convictions about issues of race and discrimination are no deeper than a water spider's footprint.

DOUBT FOUR: Your leadership. . . . By the year 2000, only 57 percent of people entering the work force will be native-born whites. White Americans have to understand that their children's standard of living is inextricably bound to the future of millions of non-white children who will pour into the work force in the next decades. Guiding them toward achievement will make America a richer, more successful society. Allowing them to self-destruct because of penny-pinching or timidity about straight talk will make

America a second-rate power. Black Americans have to believe that acquisition of skills will serve as an entry into society not because they have acquired a veneer of whiteness but because they are able. Blackness doesn't compromise ability, nor does ability compromise blackness. Both blacks and whites have to create and celebrate the common ground that binds us together as Americans and human beings.

To do that we must reach out in trust to each other. By ignoring the poverty in our cities, white Americans deny reality as much as black Americans whose sense of group identity often denies the individuality that they themselves know is God's gift to every baby. There is much to say to each other about rage and patience, about opportunity and obligation, about fear and courage, about guilt and honor. The more Americans can see beyond someone's skin to his heart and mind, the easier it will be for us to reveal our true feelings and to admit our failures as well as celebrate our strengths. The more Americans are honest about the level of distrust they hold for each other, the easier it will be to get beyond those feelings and forge a new relationship without racial overtones. . . .

The most important voice in that national dialogue is you, Mr. President. You can set us against each other or you can bring us together. You can reason with us and help us overcome deep-rooted stereotypes or you can speak in mutually contradictory sound bites and leave us at each other's throats. . . . You can push the buttons that you think give you an election or you can challenge a nation's moral conscience.

The irony here is that, as a Democrat, I am urging the Republican president to do what will serve his own party's long-term political interests. Why do I do it? Because I believe that race-baiting should be banished from politics. Because I believe communicating in code words and symbols to deliver an old shameful message should cease. There should be no more Willie Horton ads. Mr. President, will you promise not to use race again as you so shamelessly did in 1988? If you will not promise your country this, why not?

DOUBT FIVE: Your convictions. Mr. President, as vice president to Ronald Reagan you were a loyal lieutenant. To my knowledge you never expressed public opposition to anything that happened in race relations in the Reagan years. You acquiesced in giving control of the civil rights agenda to elements of the Republican Party whose southern strategy was to attract those voters who wanted to turn the clock back on race relations.

The Reagan Justice Department tried to give government tax subsidies to schools that practice racial discrimination as a matter of policy. And you went along. They were reluctant to push the Voting Rights Act renewal—and you went along. They vetoed the 1988 Civil Rights Restoration Act—and you went along. For eight years there was an assault on American civility and fair play—and you went along. On what issues would you have spoken out? Was your role as vice president more important than any conviction? Obviously, the issue of race wasn't one of them. Martin Luther King, Jr. wrote from his jail cell in Birmingham, "We will have to repent in this generation not merely for the vitriolic words and actions of bad people, but for the appalling silence of good people."

Mr. President, you saw black America fall into a deeper and deeper decline during the Reagan years. From 1984 to 1988, the number of black children murdered in America increased by 50 percent. Today, 43 percent of black children are born in poverty. And since 1984, black life expectancy has declined—the first decline for any segment of America in our history. Yet in the face of these unprecedented developments, you said and did nothing. Why did you go along?

In 1989, when you took over, you promised it would be different. But it hasn't been. The rhetoric has been softer at times, but the problem is the same. At Hampton College, a predominantly black school, you recently promised "adequate funding" for Head

Start, but three out of four eligible children are still turned away. Do you believe what you say? What is more important than getting a generation of kids on the right education track? I'm all for the important work of the Thousand Points of Light Foundation, but for it to really succeed, a president and his government must be the beacon.

Maybe you have no idea what to do about kids killing kids in our cities and people sleeping on the streets. Maybe out-of-wedlock births are outside your experience and not of importance to you. Maybe you really have concluded that urban enterprise zones and the HOPE program are a sufficient urban poverty strategy. Maybe families to you don't include white and black families living in cities, struggling to make ends meet against the same high odds that you refuse to reduce. Maybe you just don't understand. Maybe, maybe, maybe.

Who knows? We rarely hear your voice. At West Point, you exhorted America to be color-blind. But without doing something about inequity and poverty, the call for color blindness is denial and arrogance. Mr. President, you have to create a context in which a color-blind society might eventually evolve. Right now you are neither similar to the stern father administering bad news and discipline to his children, nor the wise father helping his children come to terms with emotions they don't understand or prejudices they can't conquer. And you are certainly not the leader laying out the plan and investing the political capital to change conditions. . . .

Mr. President, as you and your men dawdle in race politics, consider these facts: We will never win the global economic race if we have to carry the burden of an increasingly larger unskilled population. We will never lead the world by the example of our living values if we can't eradicate the "reservation" mentality many whites hold about our cities. We will never understand the problems of our cities—the factories closed, the housing filled with rats, the hospitals losing doctors, the schools pockmarked with bullet holes, the middle class moved away—until a white person can point out the epidemic of minority illegitimacy, drug addiction, and homicides without being charged a racist. We will never solve the problem of our cities until we intervene massively and directly to change the physical conditions of poverty and deprivation. But you can still win elections by playing on the insecurities our people feel about their jobs, their homes, their children, and their future. And so our greatest doubt about you is this: Is winning elections more important to you than unifying the country to address the problems of race and poverty that beset us?

Mr. President, this is a cry from the heart, so don't charge me with playing politics. I'm asking you to take the issue of race out of partisan politics and put it on a moral plane where healing can take place.

I believe the only way it will happen is for you to look into yourself and tell all of us what you plan to do about the issues of race and poverty in this country. Tell us why our legitimate doubts about your convictions are wrong. Tell us how you propose to make us the example of a pluralist democracy whose economy and spirit takes everyone to the higher ground. Tell us what the plan of action is for us to realize our ideals.

Tell each of us what we can do. Tell us why you think we can do it. Tell us why we must do it. Tell us, Mr. President. Lead us. Put yourself on the line. Now. Now.

ACKNOWLEDGMENTS

BILL BRADLEY GAVE ME what no United States senator ever has enough of—
time—and for that, along with his patience and forbearance as I peppered him
with questions and endlessly photographed him, I am forever grateful. Working
with Bill, watching him move effortlessly through days that would daunt the
most intrepid among us, was a lesson in grace under pressure. I owe him an
enormous debt of thanks, not the least for his trust in me and what was
exclusively my idea.

Ernestine Schlant Bradley was always a welcoming presence when I encountered her during my days in New Jersey with Bill. Though I knew before
embarking on the book that the Bradleys cherished their privacy, I am grateful
to her for her warmth and openness toward me.

Greg McCarthy, Amy Felber, Erika Gabrielsen, Perri Cartledge, and their
boss in Bill's press office, Michael Jones, were always cooperative in arranging
time for me to be with Bill. To each, especially Greg, who first heard me out
on the project and served as my earliest liaison with Bill, and to Michael, the
consummate professional, my great good thanks.

That thanks extends to the rest of Bill's Senate staff, past and present, with
whom I had contact: Marcia Aronoff for briefing me on the inner workings of

a Senate office; Rich Yurko for answering my many questions about office administration; Gene Peters for letting me glimpse the world of the legislative assistant; Ken Apfel for keeping me apprised of the Student Athlete Right-to-Know Act's progress through the legislative labyrinth; Gina Despres for her recollections of Bill's visits to the Soviet Union; Tom Bridle for additional Soviet updates; Anita Dunn for her helpful insights; Bill Foster and Wendy Pacter for describing *their* involvement with the Student Athlete Act; Jessie Leider for her scheduling wizardry; Keith Roachford for his explanatory skills; and Marina Gentilini for her gracious hospitality, even on the most hectic days.

In New Jersey, I owe a debt of thanks to Bill's state press secretary, Rona Parker, for explaining the finer points of New Jersey politics to an out-of-stater and for her very kind cooperation throughout this project; Greg Loder for keeping me logistically updated; and Hugh Drummond for describing what life is like behind the wheel of Bill's latest ancient car.

On the campaign trail I wish to thank Nick Donatiello and Bob McHugh for so generously giving me so much of their time and attention. Getting to know them both was one of the best parts of working on this book. Thanks, too, to Susan Thomases for her corroboration, and James Gray and Andy Anselmi for their advice and counsel.

Discussing Bill's campaign strategy with Michael Kaye was another high point during my research work. Michael's openness and candor with me were exemplary, and I will always cherish memories of fending off a huge crowd with him at Port Authority in New York as we talked away and watched Bill shake thousands of hands.

Many other people on Capitol Hill cooperated with me in my research for this book. I especially wish to thank Representative Ed Towns for taking time out of his busy schedule to talk to me about the origins of the Student Athlete Right-to-Know Act; Terry Hartle for regularly updating me on the bill's progress; Senator Edward M. Kennedy for allowing me to photograph him in his Labor and Human Resources office; Senate Deputy Sergeant-at-Arms Jeanine Drysdale-Lowe for explaining the Senate intern program to me; Assistant Secretary for the Majority Robert Bean and Assistant Secretary for the Minority Mary Arnold for briefing me on Senate rules and procedures; Assistant Secretary of the Senate Jeri Thomson for showing me the backstage Senate; Special Assistant for Information Systems Ray Strong and System Administrator Mark Taylor for a sense of what happens to a bill when it is introduced in the Senate; Senate Historian Richard Baker for a sense of the *structure* of Senate history; Senate Photo Historian John O. Hamilton for photo research unexcelled; former U.S. Representative from Vermont Peter Smith for his insights into Congress's innermost workings; House Education Committee staffers Colleen Thompson, Patty Sullivan, and Ricardo Martinez for explaining the House's response to the Student Athlete Right-to-Know Act; and Mark Abraham of the *Newark Star-Ledger* for making an outsider feel welcome among the Washington press photographers' corps.

Elsewhere, my thanks go to Ellen Morgenstern and Stefanie Christopoulos of WWOR-TV Channel 9 in Secaucus, New Jersey, for arranging my press pass to the first campaign debate; Ron Nief, public affairs director at Middlebury College for letting me observe its commencement celebration; Gary Johnson of the NCAA for answering my phone call; Ken Dautrich of the Eagleton Institute of Politics at Rutgers University for important polling information; Robert Schoelkopf at the Marine Mammal Stranding Center in Brigantine, New Jersey, for his insights into Bill's environmental concerns; Steve Chambers of the *Asbury Park Press* for his views on Bill as a senator and a person; Dick Cook in Crystal City, Missouri, for his reminiscences about Bill's childhood; Professor Barry Scherr at Dartmouth College for eleventh-hour translation help; and Dick Barnett, Alaa Abdulnaby, Dr. Joel H. Fish, and Bob Hurley at Bill's student athlete seminar, for thoughts, recollections, and anecdotes.

Allyn Johnston at Harcourt Brace Jovanovich is a genius at helping authors find the right *approach* into a book, as well as coaxing a manuscript into an acceptable state. Her gentle yet rigorous editing of my prose improved both its quality and my appreciation of what an outstanding editor can do for a book. I cannot think of anyone else with whom I would rather have worked. Others at HBJ whom I would like to thank are Bonnie Verburg for being the first to say yes to this project; and Louise Howton, Liz Bicknell, Trina Stahl, Anna Roach, Susànn Cokal, and Barry Age for their many design and editorial contributions.

As always, Henry Dunow was a wonderful agent, counsel, sounding-board, and, most important, friend. As one who needs frequent encouragement, I continue to appreciate Henry's faith, inspiration, and example.

My wife, Pam, and our sons, Andrew and Sam, kept our household working while I made my numerous trips to Washington and New Jersey. When I read chapters aloud for their critique, their comments were always thoughtful and encouraging, and when I wrenched my back during a family visit to Washington, Pam took over all logistical duties while my sons became my camera bearers and crutches. "What a beautiful family you have!" Bill Bradley exclaimed to me after meeting them. I could not have said it any better.

NOTES

CHAPTER 2: "BACKGROUND"

Pages 8–9 through quote ending ". . . a little boy." See McPhee, John, *A Sense of Where You Are* (New York: The Noonday Press, 1965, 1978), p. 66–72.

Page 10: "It was a reserved house . . . schoolwork." As reported by John L. Phillips in his profile on Bradley as a senatorial candidate, *The New York Times Magazine*, June 18, 1978, p. 17.

Pages 10–11: McPhee, pp. 66–72.

Page 11: "It was simple . . . things about myself." As reported by Phillips, p. 17.

Pages 11–14 (top): McPhee, pp. 72–79.

Page 14: "Oh, sure . . . they fell off." As reported by Phillips, p. 17.

Page 14: "In a stirring . . . the deep South." See Halter, Jon C., *Bill Bradley: One to Remember* (New York: G. P. Putnam's Sons, 1975), p. 21.

Page 16: ". . . something really important . . . because of it." As reported by Phillips, p. 17.

Page 16: "For the time being . . ." to end of page. See McPhee, pp. 123–140.

Page 17: "Conrad's view . . . stop-drift mechanisms are." As reported by Phillips, p. 17.

Page 19, (last paragraph): See Hirshey, Gerri, "Bradley's Time," *Rolling Stone*, June 14, 1990, p. 66.

Page 21: "I was always . . . view of politics derives from that." As reported by Phillips, p. 17.

Page 21: For an inside view of how Bradley "looked at America," see his *Life on the Run* (New York: Quadrangle Books, 1976).

Page 21: "looking at America." See Phillips, p. 74.

Pages 22–23: See McPhee, p. 206; Phillips, pp. 17–76; "A Senate Scorecard," *Newsweek*, October 16, 1978, p. 78.

CHAPTER 3: "ON BEING A UNITED STATES SENATOR"

Page 28 (last paragraph)–29: See Rothenberg, Randall, "Bradley in Washington," *New Jersey Monthly*, March 1981, pp. 50–51.

Page 31: "The core of both experiences . . . quickly as a senator." From a televised interview between Bill Bradley and Arthur Ashe titled "The Pursuit of Excellence," aired on ESPN, December 17, 1987.

Page 33: See Rothenberg, pp. 48, 51, 81.

Pages 33–34: For those readers who wish to read an in-depth examination of the 1986 Tax Reform Act, I recommend *Showdown at Gucci Gulch* by Jeffrey H. Birnbaum and Alan S. Murray (New York: Vintage Books, 1987).

CHAPTER 6: "THE BIRTH OF A LAW: PART II"

Page 66: "I am very pleased . . . not covered by NCAA regulations." As reported by William C. Rhoden, "N.C.A.A. Stiffens Practice and Season Limits," *The New York Times*, p. D25.

CHAPTER 7: "A DAY"

Pages 74–75: Some information on the Bradleys' domestic arrangements and the quote from Ernestine Bradley are as reported by Mary-Lou Weisman, "The Bradley Bunch," *Woman's Day*, February 6, 1990, pp. 52, 54.

Page 76: "a legal document . . . among nations by consensus." From Castelle, Kay, *In the Child's Best Interest: A Primer on the U.N. Convention on the Rights of the Child* (New York: Foster Parents Plan International, Inc., 1989), p. 3.

CHAPTER 8: "THE SOVIETS"

Page 98: "We should be . . . debt problem of the 1980s." Bill Bradley, as interviewed on "The MacNeil-Lehrer NewsHour," December 13, 1988.

Pages 100–101: See Bradley, Bill, "Time to Help the Republics," *The Washington Post*, August 28, 1991. p. A23.

CHAPTER 13: "CAMPAIGN: PART I"

Page 154: See Kerr, Peter, "Bradley, Though Popular, Chases Re-election on Tiptoe," *The New York Times*, May 30, 1990, p. B1.

CHAPTER 14: "CAMPAIGN: PART II"

Pages 171–172: See "Election Survey," *The Somerset County Courier-News*, October 24, 1990, p. A1.

CHAPTER 15: "ELECTION"

Page 181: "They don't believe . . . any control over." As reported by David S. Broder, "Near defeat teaches Bradley to risk," *The Burlington (Vt.) Free Press*, December 2, 1990, p. 4E.

EPILOGUE

Page 185: "that it might be over tomorrow . . . say it." As reported by Thomas B. Edsall, "Bradley Confronts Volatile Issues of Race and Rights," *The Washington Post*, July 17, 1991, p. A15.

FURTHER READING

Three essential works for readers interested in Bill Bradley's pre-Senate life are his own *Life on the Run* (New York: Quadrangle/New York Times Book Co., 1976; New York: Bantam Books, Inc., 1977 [paperback]), *A Sense of Where You Are: A Profile of Bill Bradley at Princeton* by John McPhee (New York: Farrar, Straus and Giroux, Inc., 1965, 1978), and *Bill Bradley: One to Remember* by Jon C. Halter (New York: Putnam Publishing Group, 1975).

Helpful in-depth studies of the legislative process and how Congress works include *The Legislative Process in the United States* by Malcolm E. Jewell and Samuel C. Patterson (New York: Random House, Inc., 1977), *How Congress Works* by Dan Radler (New York: NAL Books, 1976), and *How Congress Works* by Congressional Quarterly, Inc. staff (Washington, D.C.: Congressional Quarterly, 1991).

Among the many popular discussions of Washington politics, one of the best is *The Power Game: How Washington Really Works* by Hedrick Smith (New York: Random House, Inc., 1988).

There are numerous biographies and studies of modern senators and representatives. Three standouts are *Robert Kennedy and His Times* by Arthur M.

Schlesinger, Jr. (New York: Ballantine Books, Inc., 1985), *Clare Booth Luce* by Wilfrid Sheed (New York: Berkley Publishing Group, 1984), and *The Making of a Senator: Dan Quayle* by Richard F. Fenno (Washington, D.C.: Congressional Quarterly, 1988).

For an understanding of congressional history see *The Senate of the United States* by Senate Historian Richard Allan Baker and *The United States House of Representatives* by James T. Currie (both Malabar, Florida: Krieger Publishing Co., 1988). Two handsomely illustrated overviews of Senate history are *The Senate 1789–1989: Addresses on the History of the United States Senate* by Senator Robert C. Byrd (2 volumes, Washington, D.C.: The U.S. Government Printing Office, 1988, 1991; 2 additional volumes to be published by 1994), and *Historic Almanac of the United States Senate* by Senator Robert Dole (Washington, D.C.: The U.S. Government Printing Office, 1989).

INDEX

Numbers in *italics* refer to pages with illustrations.